A DAY IN THE
BLEACHERS

A DAY IN THE BLEACHERS

ARNOLD HANO

Introduction by Roger Kahn

DA CAPO PRESS
A Member of the Perseus Books Group

Cataloging-in-Publication data for this book is available from the Library of Congress.

This Da Capo Press paperback edition of *A Day in the Bleachers* is an unabridged republication of the first edition supplemented with a new introduction and new photographs to replace the original drawings. First published in 1955, it is reprinted by arrangement with the author.

ISBN 0–306–81322–X

Published by Da Capo Press
A Member of the Perseus Books Group
http://www.dacapopress.com

Da Capo Press books are available at special discounts for bulk purchases in the U.S. by corporations, institutions, and other organizations. For more information, please contact the Special Markets Department at the Perseus Books Group, 11 Cambridge Center, Cambridge, MA 02142, or call (800) 255-1514 or (617) 252-5298, or e-mail special.markets@perseusbooks.com.

1 2 3 4 5 6 7 8 9—07 06 05 04

For Bonnie
My Favorite Giant Fan
with Love

A NEW FOREWORD TO THE
50TH ANNIVERSARY EDITION

Not many weeks after the New York Giants clobbered the heavily favored Cleveland Indians in four straight games of the 1954 World Series, I received a phone call from a good friend, Arnold Hano. He and his wife, Bonnie, a tiny Iowan, wanted Phyllis and me to come over to his West Side Manhattan apartment for supper.

"I'd like to show you something I've just written," said Arnold, who spoke then, as he still does, as rapidly as a Roger Clemens fastball.

The "something" turned out to be the book that you have in your hand at this moment. On that first reading of *A Day in the Bleachers* in Arnold's apartment, I recall two things clearly. One, Arnold hovered over my shoulder, nervously and expectantly. Two, I loved every line of his little book.

The world has turned over many times since Arnold went on his serendipitous writing adventure. The Polo Grounds are no more, of course, having been replaced by public housing (it is my sad guess that few of the occupants care that the ineffable Willie Mays once played on what is now their home). The Giants, too, have been transplanted to San Francisco, where a columnist wrote years ago that his town was the one place "they boo Willie Mays and cheer Khrushchev." Many of the Giants who took part in the 1954 series are also gone, including their strident manager, Leo Durocher, catcher Wes Westrum, and pitcher Sal Maglie. Vic Wertz, the Indians' big slugger, who banged the ball that Willie turned into a legend, is also gone.

Happily, Willie, now in his seventies, is still with us, as is Arnold Hano. In Laguna Beach, California, in his restless retirement, Arnold still pays close attention to the pennant races and waits for another Willie Mays to come along.

It's fitting that Arnold should have written about a classic Polo Grounds afternoon, for he grew up with the Giants when men such as manager John McGraw paced impatiently in the Giants' dugout. The heroes of the day were such men as "The Meeker Marvel" Carl Hubbell and, from Gretna, Louisiana, "The Boy Wonder"—Master Mel Ott. Arnold may have missed those early twentieth-century icons Christy Mathewson and "Iron Man" Joe McGinnity, but he had his own latter-day favorites in Willie Mays, Bobby Thomson, and Monte Irvin.

One point about the author that must be noted: he never sat in a reserved seat or a press box until he became a professional sportswriter—or, to put it more accurately, an eclectic journalist writing about everything from migraine headaches to Mickey Rooney to Marlon Brando. The writer who was to become the National Sportscasters and Sportswriters Association "Man of the Year" in 1964 had always been a bleachers guy, priding himself on inhabiting that blue-collar venue. Remember, when you sat on those Polo Grounds bleacher planks, you were probably more than 500 feet from home plate—or at least it seemed that far. But that didn't stop Arnold and his bleacher confederates from calling balls and strikes from their perch, belligerently challenging the eyesight of the umpire working behind the plate. And as for the famous Mays catch that September afternoon, Arnold probably had a better perspective on it than almost anyone else in the ballpark.

As you read *A Day in the Bleachers* you will notice—and this is for the sake of full disclosure—that I am quoted in its pages twice, both times accurately. Yes, as the book states, I did give up on the Giants fifty-nine times that year of 1954, which was, of course, the exact number of games the Giants lost. And long before everyone began to hit sixty home runs or more a year, I referred to Babe Ruth's sixty home runs of 1927 as "sacrosanct." How times change!

When I first met Arnold Hano at a small New York publishing house more than fifty years ago, I started to call him "Judge." I still do. The nickname came about because I thought his last name was really Hand, not Hano, which brought the famous Judge Learned Hand immediately to mind. And as I mentioned earlier, Arnold has always spoken in rapid-fire style, like a 2003 version of Floyd Gibbons.

Well, he writes just as quickly. I don't think that I'll be telling tales out of school by revealing that he wrote *Bleachers* in about the same time as it takes most people to run a marathon—yet he managed to turn a half-dozen hours on a bleachers pew into a tight-knit masterpiece. The book, in my mind, is a gem of clarity and honest observation, a tribute to Arnold's reporting skills. He rarely engages in the hyperbole or overembellishment so characteristic of many sportswriters. I do not exaggerate when I say he belongs right up there with many of the best sports scribblers of the '30s, '40s, and '50s— men such as Red Smith, Frank Graham, Jimmy Cannon, Bill Heinz, John Lardner, and Paul Gallico. It is only a pity that Arnold never banged on his typewriter for a daily newspaper.

When Arnold took the subway that day in 1954, he hadn't the slightest notion he was going to write a book about the experience. All along he thought he might get a magazine article out of it, which is basically what he did in those days. But as the game progressed, he found himself scrawling notes in the margin of his *New York Times*. Needless to say, he wrote his reminders furiously when Willie made his famous catch.

"What the hell are you writing?" one of Arnold's fellow bleacher-sitters asked him at one stage.

"Just putting down my blood pressure," answered the Judge.

Unfortunately, Arnold never saved that priceless copy of the *Times* for his personal archives—but he does have the scorecard that he conscientiously kept that afternoon (Baseball Hall of Fame, take notice!).

When owner Horace Stoneham left the Polo Grounds and all those diehard Giants fans in 1957 to relocate his club to San Francisco, Arnold and I took it personally. Arnold swore at the time that he would never speak of the Giants again as long as he lived. I'm sure other Giants adherents shared the same sentiment. But we *did* join a dispirited group of less than 11,000 fans that masochistically attended the Giants' farewell game at the old Harlem ballpark. Naturally, we chose to sit in the bleachers—and as Arnold remembers it—almost the same spot from which Arnold had watched the 1954 game.

Some of the holdovers from that saga of '54 were still in Giants uniforms, including Willie, Dusty Rhodes, Wes Westrum, Johnny Antonelli, and Whitey Lockman. But Bill Rigney had replaced Durocher as manager, so he was in charge during those last painful moments at the Polo Grounds.

As Arnold and I looked around at those melancholy occupants of the bleachers, we wondered how many of them might have seen Willie's catch and throw just a few years before—and was it possible that maybe a few of them had read Arnold's book?

This valedictory game, against the Pittsburgh Pirates, was a dismal event. "It was the saddest damn thing I've even seen," said Arnold. Maybe only a death in the family could have seemed worse. The Giants lost, 9–1. My recollection is that Willie didn't even get one measly hit. When the unseemly exhibition finally came to an end, the souvenir collectors—"scavengers" would be a better word to describe them—stormed the ball field, like so many ants unleashed. They tore plots of grass out of the diamond, ripped the bases loose, walked off with advertising signs. If they could have, they would have hauled off the dugouts. The thought occurred to us that Arnold should have carted off the bleacher plank that had helped him memorialize one of the undying moments of baseball history. But he didn't.

The whole crazy scene put me in mind of something I'd heard about years before—when voyeuristic spectators went berserk at matinee idol Rudolph Valentino's funeral in midtown Manhattan in 1925. Or the ghouls who searched the site of football coach Knute Rockne's plane crash in Bazaar, Kansas, in 1931, madly looking for remnants of Rockne's belongings.

On the subway home Arnold and I confessed to each other that we would never again give our hearts or our ticket money to another baseball team. But within the year the two of us were listening to the San Francisco Giants' games late at night, via the artful Les Keiter's reconstruction on the radio.

After all, there was still Willie Mays to cheer for.

Ray Robinson
January 2004

INTRODUCTION

When this book first appeared in the enchanted island of the 1950s, I was struck both by Arnold Hano's writing style and his daring. The writing is what amateurs call effortless. Reading *A Day in the Bleachers*, you concentrate on the day, the game, the ball players, the fans, without much awareness of a man at a typewriter grunting and straining through the non-anesthetized labor that precedes the birth of a book. The scene and Mr. Hano's comments simply flow. Everyone who has written seriously knows that sustaining a flowing style is as effortless as cleaning the Augean stables with a water pistol.

Then Mr. Hano presumed to cast an entire book within the time frame of the day of this game. It was an exceptionally exciting game, particularly for Giant fans, a breed Hano champions with naked—Brooklynites would say pornographic—enthusiasm. But how, wondered some of us who wrote for newspapers in those days, could you find enough in one baseball game to create a book? Mr. Hano's success made that question moot.

More than a quarter century later, I re-approached *A Day in the Bleachers* apprehensively. Certain books, certain poems better with age. Others do not. Particularly in non-fiction, styles and attitudes alter with the seasons; and perspective, a sense of history, clears our vision. Yesteryear's vivid and successful non-fiction book can age as gracelessly as a New York City taxi. It is a dangerous business returning to old favorites; too often you find they are not your favorites anymore.

How, then, does *A Day in the Bleachers* survive? I found it richer and more rewarding in the disco-Steinbrenner-instant-replay 1980s than I did so very long ago. Yes, I thought, this was how it was to go to a ball game once. This was what it was like to sit in the cheap seats and follow a ball game as a knowledgeable fan. This was how it was when Willie Mays was young and all the grass was real and the bleachers were a haven, rather than a place of menace where strange young people throw golf balls at the heads of visiting outfielders.

I have not simply sentimentalized the past, I thought. There really was a 1954.

❋   ❋   ❋

Since the original publication of *A Day in the Bleachers*, almost everything the book represents has changed or vanished. The Polo Grounds, that great, green horseshoe of a ball park, where the story unfolds, has been torn down. Public housing now rises from soil that felt the spikes of Mathewson and Hubbell. The New York Giants, the team of John McGraw and later Durocher, Maglie, Bobby Thomson and Willie Mays, moved to San Francisco after the season of 1957. Unlike the Dodgers, the Giants have not been able to synthesize a strong new California identity. In the early 1980s, they are simply one more ball club, one out of 26, mostly anonymous, like the Atlanta Braves or the Toronto Blue Jays.

Without knowing it, Hano was catching a team at the

peak moment of its existence. Who could have imagined after 1954, when Hano's favorites swept the World Series from the Cleveland Indians, that the New York Giants had but three years of life? Certainly not fans, who, like Mr. Hano, rooted their heroes home.

A leveled stadium and a ball club wrenched 3,000 miles from familiar scenes remind you that the winds of change blow fiercely. But Hano's book, far from fierce, is a subtle interweaving of two concurrent events. One is the ball game on the field. The other is the experience of going to that game amid a crowd of strangers in a time before televised sports became a national addiction. Mr. Hano, something of a purist, even expresses quiet contempt for those who brought portable radios into the Polo Grounds. A generation of us felt the same. "Hey, whatsa matter, Mac. You need a radio announcer to tell you three strikes is out?"

I read once where a conductor complained that "people now take a shower while listening to Beethoven's Ninth." He was protesting a diminution, indeed a trivializing, of human experience. Listening to the Ninth Symphony was once a rare and special occasion, for which one prepared and which one remembered years afterward. In much the same way television works against the old magic of the World Series. You no longer have to struggle to find a ticket, part with cash, worry about the location of your seat, and hope passionately that it does not rain. Pull a knob and a replica of the game appears in your living room. Children now grow up on electronic baseball.

Although the sixth game of the 1981 World Series was the highest-rated television program of its week, no one saw the complete ballgame on TV. It is a measure of baseball's subtlety that the diamond cannot be compressed to fit a picture tube. The field is too large. The participants are too widely spaced. The baseball itself is too small for ideal television. When we watch at home, we see a fractional sliver of a game and we cannot even determine for ourselves what fraction we are to see. The cameras become our eyes. The director determines what portion of the action appears.

Nor do we have to pay very close attention. The good plays are re-run over and over. Did you miss Graig Nettles's diving snare? No matter. You'll see it again and again, from different angles, as electronics warps the reality of time.

When you read Hano's classic description of Willie Mays's classic Series catch, a suspenseful panorama unfolds. Vic Wertz swings. Mays turns his head and runs. The ball describes its arc—either a long low fly or a very high line drive. Two base runners move. The game, perhaps the Series, hangs in an exquisite balance.

Like Hano, I saw the catch and the throw that followed. In the moments afterward, I felt nothing except shock. Mays had surpassed my understanding of what a ball player could do. Seeing the same play on television is very different. Mays runs as he did, but the ball is out of sight. When it does appear for an instant, it is a tiny blur, vanishing into a shrunken glove. The marvelous confluence of Wertz's high drive in flight and Willie Mays in flight is absent. You might as well hear Beethoven's Ninth while taking a shower.

Not only is your commitment and some of the action missing, the other fans are missing too. Once you find a seat at a ball park, you become part of a group experience. You have your favorite team and players. The other fans have theirs. A spirited competition develops among the strangers who are suddenly part of the same crowd. Whose champions will succeed? Who in the crowd is wisest in the ways of baseball?

Hano gives us a lovely moment when someone shouts at

a Cleveland batter named Dave Pope, "Hit it where you live." Pope comes from Pennsylvania. Foul territory, Hano notes.

Watching in a living room destroys competitive rooting. Manners prevail. The fans' expertise is pre-empted by announcers who may, or may not, know what they're talking about. Your concentration is broken by commercials and advertisements for football games and motorcycle races that the network will televise next week-end.

Going to a ball game is an active, if not a physical, experience. Watching a televised ball game is as passive as monitoring Johnny Carson between two sets of toes.

I would no more argue for outlawing televised baseball than I would argue for dismantling the interstate highway system. These things exist and bring certain benefits. More people watch the Series now, and you can drive from Albany to Chicago without having to stop for traffic lights. But it is important to recognize that technological innovation creates not only progress but a kind of loss.

*   *   *

In the middle 1960s, ten years after Hano's book, someone invented the phrase "new journalism." It was catchy, commercial, and accurate in a limited way. Orthodox old journalism steadfastly denied the importance of the journalist. You were not to intrude yourself into your stories and if there was one sin greater than inaccuracy it was using the vertical pronoun, "I."

Stanley Woodward, the famous sports editor of the New York Herald Tribune, once insisted that an apprentice writer was beyond redemption. "How can you be sure," I said, "He's only 22." Woodward glowered. "He single spaces his copy and he uses the first person." (As a matter of fact, the writer in question subsequently enrolled himself in law school.)

New journalists were encouraged to write "I." Further, they were urged, in different words, to treat their stories as personal encounters. Editors who called this approach "new" were incorrect. The past is rich in examples of personal essays and encounter journalism. But the popularity of the approach, and its general acceptance, were a departure.

The form is decidedly fragile. One can overuse "I," until the reader is turned off by what he perceives as the writer's ego. Then, for an encounter to work, the journalist has to make himself an interesting person on the printed page. Who wants to read the encounters of a dullard?

Now here is Hano, in 1955 publishing a book in which he says "I," when he means "I," and where a baseball game becomes a crucial experience in the life of Arnold Hano. A question, then, is why *A Day in the Bleachers* did not win more attention and, coincidentally, all the sales that were its due.

In the 1950s, a prominent author announced, "Don't waste your time with sports books. They never sell." In publishing, a trendy business, editors believed the same thing. There is a significant element of self-fulfilling prophecy in the attention a book achieves.

If a publisher believes a book can be a best-seller, he takes steps to convert belief to truth. Advertise. Send the author about to appear on radio and television programs. Get copies of the book into the hands of columnists, other authors and people of prominence who read. In short, get the book talked about. This doesn't always work, of course, and there are rare instances of books published quietly that succeed on sheer merit. (*Cry, the Beloved Country* is a notable instance.) But without loud banging of publicity drums few books really have a chance.

Hano published against the conventional wisdom that

there was only a tiny market for sports books, a wisdom that has been laid bare as ignorance. First came *The Long Season,* a diary of one major league year, compiled by a literate pitcher named Jim Brosnan. It carried halfway up the New York Times best-seller list. Bill Veeck's life story, *Veeck as in Wreck,* composed with Ed Linn, had another excellent run. Jerry Kramer of the Green Bay Packers and Jim Bouton, the former Yankee pitcher, published diaries, edited by professional journalists, that became major best-sellers in subsequent years.

In 1972 a book I called *The Boys of Summer* led the Times list for several months and five years later I cracked the list again with a baseball journey titled *A Season in the Sun.* Finally, and most relevant to *A Day in the Bleachers,* is the work of Roger Angell, who writes baseball pieces for the *New Yorker* magazine. Two collections of Angell's articles—*The Summer Game* and *Five Seasons*—have gained both attention and royalties unimaginable for a sports book of the 1950s. Angell's approach is to cast himself as a man in the grandstand, which brings us back to Hano and the bleachers.

They did not build bleachers in the new multi-sport stadiums in St. Louis, Atlanta, Cincinnati. The old bleachers were uncovered stands, where fans sat on wooden benches on leisurely afternoons in the summer sun. This book is about the bleachers, the people on the wooden benches and the ball players beyond. It is about a time and a team and a ball park that are gone. It is the first, and perhaps the best, of all the books written from the point of view of the man in the stands and I am glad to see it get a second chance.

—ROGER KAHN
New York City
November, 1981

ONE

When the evening papers of September 28, 1954, reported that a dozen men and boys were already camping across the street from the bleacher entrance outside the Polo Grounds prior to the first World Series contest, I felt the urge.

I turned to my wife and said, "I think I'll go to the game tomorrow."

She said, "Don't you need a ticket?"

I said, "Only for the reserved seats. I'll sit in the bleachers."

She snorted. My wife has three ways of showing disapproval. She harangues loud and long when she is not very sure of her position. Or she may be entirely silent when she is terribly sure. This is usually an act of kindness on her part, as though she were dealing with a dumb animal. Or, lastly, she may snort. This means, I have at last learned, that she disagrees, that she thinks I'm a dumb animal, and by God, kindness can go just so far.

I said, "Is there something you want me to do around

the house instead? You have a particularly heavy dish you want me to wash, is that it? Or a window to open?"

"Oh, no," she said, "it's not that. It's just that you'll never get in. And if you do, you'll never be able to see anything."

I am a man of even temperament and I have sat in the Polo Grounds bleachers many times. I like to sit in the Polo Grounds bleachers. When I was four years old, my family used to live in a big red brick apartment house on Edgecomb Avenue, across the street from the Polo Grounds. My grandfather Ike was a lieutenant on the New York police force. He had a season pass to the Polo Grounds. It was a simple matter for my mother to get me off her hands by teaching me how to cross streets by myself. I was "shipped off" to the Polo Grounds the way other boys are sent to camp every summer, except my summer began in the middle of April and extended to the end of September. Thus at four years of age, I saw approximately seventy-seven baseball games.

But even then I knew something was lacking. There I sat, by myself, in the grandstand, white shirt, blue-knit tie, brown suede jacket. I had been told to behave myself, so I did. I became a student of the game—even before I became a fan. I did not scream my hoarse—or, then, piping —advice to Manager McGraw. I did not chortle in amusement when pink-cheeked Mel Ott played his first game and raised his right leg high in the air as he started his swing. I enjoyed myself, but I was not thrilled. When I got home every afternoon, the elevator man would ask me, "How was the game today?" I would answer, "It was fine, sir."

Now, that's just not baseball.

So one Saturday the following spring, I tucked the pass in my pocket and with fifty cents that I had scraped together from selling *Colliers* and the *Woman's Home Com-*

2

Photo: TCMA

Willie Mays, center fielder

panion, I bought myself a bleacher seat. I do not know why I was so impelled, but I must have heard from the older boys about sitting in the bleachers. I do not remember the game or who won, but I do remember that I *was* thrilled. And after a few more such Saturdays I was able to join in the raucous laughter when Ott *did* raise his right leg and somebody yelled, "All right, Otty, I wanna hear ya bark." I had no idea what he meant, but I laughed, as loud and coarsely as I could. All I know is that I had a helluva good time.

Later, as I got older and money became scarcer, I took to ripping holes in the pockets of the knickers I was wearing. Then I'd go up to the ball game, sit in the bleachers, and pick up all the stray soda bottles. I'd drop them through the holes in my pockets, ten to fifteen bottles in each pocket, and the bottles would settle about my knees and upward inside my pants. The forty to sixty cents I got back in bottle deposits paid for most of my day's expenses.

Still later, in my early adulthood, I went through a period of extreme embarrassment about sitting in the bleachers. My friends, who sat in reserved seats, used to think I was a tightwad or eccentric. So for a brief spell I sat in the reserved seats and felt uncomfortable. Everybody is so polite. I am a vicarious thrill-seeker, and I respond to baseball games in a childish, almost nasty way. My wife says I am a vindictive man when it comes to baseball; I believe she is right. In the bleachers, however, you can be vindictive. Nearly everybody else is.

So when my wife told me I would not get in and if I did, I wouldn't see anything, I felt like telling her about the one time I sat in a box seat between home and first. It was awful. I could see everybody's face very clearly, but I had no idea of what was really going on, the pattern of play as it folds and unfolds and makes baseball the con-

4

stantly shifting and exciting vista it is. But I know she would have considered this sour grapes.

So I said, "I think I will get in." I ignored the business about not seeing.

My wife seized upon this. "All right, go," she said. "But take the portable radio with you. You might as well know what's happening."

It was, of course, her way of getting in the last word. We do not own a portable radio.

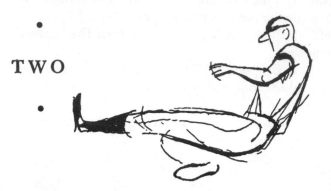

TWO

I had not attended a World Series contest since the fourth game of the 1936 series, between the Giants and the Yankees. That game was played in the Yankee Stadium and took place on either a Saturday or a Sunday. Had I called that game to mind, I would have had no trouble about getting in to this, the first game of the 1954 series, between the Giants and the Cleveland Indians. I would have got up at the crack of dawn.

On that day, as I remember it now, over eighteen years ago, I went with my brother and a friend of ours, a Yankee fan. The friend knew the Stadium bleachers better than we did, so we let him lead the way. The Yankee Stadium bleachers accommodate about fifteen thousand people. We got to the ball park around eight in the morning, or some five hours before game time. When we got inside, we found the place packed. A few minutes later and we would not have got in at all. Not that I would have minded. It was a terrible day. The Giants lost, 5-2 as I recall, and their pitcher, Carl Hubbell, one of my favorite ball players at that time, was knocked out of the box. I remember that I cried when he walked from the mound.

So if the Yankee Stadium bleachers were filled a little

after eight, what would happen on this day if the school-boys decided to go to the game? True, the game was to be played on a Wednesday, but in 1954, Rosh Hashana fell on Tuesday and Wednesday. When I was a boy this Jewish holiday meant a general exodus for ball fields or down-town movie houses.

But I am ever an optimist and often a fool. I let my hopes rest on the fact that nearly everybody today owns a television set and could see the game in his or her living room. We do not own a television set.

So, despite the slight trepidation arising from those twelve people camping overnight, I set the alarm for the not unlikely time of seven-thirty the next morning. World Series overnight campers are habitually ignorant of base-ball, and a dozen fools, braving the weather bureau re-ports of probable thunder showers, did not mean the tiny bleacher section would overflow well before game time. And even pre-series camping seems to be less of a mania than it used to be.

I can remember when the first fans would line up ten days before the opening game of the series. Now it has been reduced to a few people arriving one evening to see a game the next afternoon. They seem to do it just to pre-serve some idiotic convention and provide the newspapers with what is exaggeratedly called "human interest." I took further heart in the remark attributed to one of the over-night fans who was asked by a reporter which team he was rooting for, the Giants or the Indians.

"Neither," he snarled, "I hate 'em both. I'm here only because I haven't missed a World Series opener in twenty-seven years."

And so when the alarm went off the next morning, I viewed the thick morning haze with pleasure. Others would

7

be scared off. I showered and had a leisurely breakfast, kissed my wife, and prepared to leave. Then just as I opened the outside door, she said, "Do you want my opera glasses?"

I said, "No," and left. I did not slam the door.

My wife has come to baseball only in recent years. For a while she was a Dodger fan because she lived in East Flatbush and thought only players hailing from the designated city-name were allowed on a club's roster. It is probably good that the changes of franchise that sent the Braves from Boston to Milwaukee and the Browns (Orioles) from St. Louis to Baltimore occurred after she had acquired greater knowledge about the sport. As it is, she still considers such changes "unnatural."

"Unnatural" is one of my wife's favorite words. She becomes very upset when a ball player is traded from one city to another, especially if he is married. When Bobby Thomson was traded to Milwaukee, she fumed for weeks. She would have become a Milwaukee fan as a result were it not for the fact that I persuaded her that Milwaukee was equally guilty of the unnatural crime of uprooting the Thomson family from Staten Island and shipping it halfway across the United States.

She is now a Giant fan, but mostly because she hears their names more than those of any other club. We listen to night games over our radio and on occasion go to one. The first game she ever saw was in 1952 when the Giants defeated the St. Louis Cardinals, 3-1. I remember with amusement that she screamed in delight after the third out in the top half of the ninth inning. Throughout the game she had been silent, and at one point when Henry Thompson hit a long drive heading in the direction of the right-field seats, she remained seated while everybody else stood up.

Then as I sat down, she said, "Did it go in?"

Henry Thompson, third baseman

I said, "Yes," and she nodded, quite happy.

It is a philosophy that rules out listening to election results. "Why stay up all night?" she says. "You can read about it tomorrow."

Nobody else acts that way at a game. When it is over, they just get up and leave, either happy or dejected. She feels that she has come to see the Giants win and once the game is official and they *have* won, *then* she must scream her joy.

I like going to the games with my wife. It is an interesting experience. I also like not going with my wife.

On this morning, I weighed the alternate means of transportation to the ball park. I could walk over from Broadway where we live to Central Park West, three longish blocks, and take the Independent Subway. Or I could walk two quite short blocks to the Broadway IRT station, go down to 59th Street and then tranfer to the Independent Line and ride up to the Polo Grounds stop. In one case it meant a a long walk and a short ride; the other was vice-versa. I chose the short walk.

And so it was a few minutes before nine that I boarded the "D" train of the Independent Line (the 8th Avenue Line, as most New Yorkers call it, although it runs on 8th *and* the Avenue of the Americas which most New Yorkers call 6th Avenue) and took my seat. The "D" train is an express that carries Bronxites to downtown New York on its southerly route, and, it seems to me, baseball fans to the Polo Grounds on its northerly trip. When I boarded the train, I noted with satisfaction that it was relatively empty.

The bleacher gates had been originally scheduled to open at ten o'clock, but a few days before the first game, the newspapers duly reported a time change to nine. No one mentioned why the change had occurred, but I should once more have realized that this was a fact in concert with

10

others. Had I done so, I might either have stayed home or else got up even before that crack of dawn. I know now that the opening of the gates was shifted from ten to nine simply because the Giant management was wise to the fact that there was going to be quite a crowd of people trying to get in to the game. And I should have known it then.

For one thing, the Giants are a more popular ball club than most people realize. Of course, in the days between the last few pennants (those drought years of 1938 through 1950, and again 1952 and 1953), attendance at the ball park sloughed off, but this is because a losing team seldom enjoys good box office.

Exceptions to this rule are the huge crowds that entertained and were occasionally entertained by the Milwaukee Braves in 1953 and 1954, and the Baltimore Orioles in 1954. The Braves finished third both seasons which is good, but not terrifically so, and the Orioles seventh in 1954 (to the surprise of many experts who did not think the Philadelphia Athletics were quite that bad), but each team drew enormous throngs.

However, unlike the Braves in Milwaukee or the Orioles in Baltimore, the Giants have been around New York and the Harlem River for many years, and Giant fans, maltreated by poor teams in the past fifteen years, have nursed their bruised spirits in taverns and living rooms before radio and, more recently, television sets, rather than at the Polo Grounds. But the fans exist. They merely go into hiding when things are too terrible to bear.

This season, however, the Giants had astonished the nation's onlookers and sports-page readers when they occupied first place in the middle of June, a position they were to hold right through the final day of the National League pennant campaign.

The year 1954 was a peculiar season. For most of the

11

season the Brooklyn Dodgers seemed to be the better team and apparently it was only a matter of time before they would straighten themselves out and slap down the Giants. On three separate occasions, despite my loyalty and blazing hopes, I gave up on the Giants and their pennant chances. Most Giant fans did the same. A friend of mine, Ray Robinson (no, not the fighter) gave up on the Giants fifty-nine times by actual count, or the number of times they lost during the pennant race of 1954. I couldn't really blame him.

After all, this was pretty much the same Giant team that had finished thirty-five games out of first place in 1953. It did not seem possible that Mays and Antonelli would make that much difference. And the Dodgers, with Don Newcombe back, seemed, on paper, even stronger than they had in '53. But there is a law that doesn't really exist, the law of averages, and in 1954 it made itself apparent with almost eerie regularity, so regularly in fact as to prove the non-existence of the law of averages.

The Giants, as I have viewed them with what I admit is a prejudiced eye, have been an unlucky team for ten or fifteen years. (True, in 1951 they seemed lucky when they won a pennant that the same Dodgers had all but wrapped up. However, it was not so much luck as it was astonishingly effective pitching that won the pennant for the Giants in 1951, plus a Dodger collapse that must be unmatched in major-league history.) In all the other years, Giant hitters, as I sat in pained silence, would hit savage line drives drawn as if by magnetism to a waiting glove. Opposing teams would hit pop flies that would fall unmolested and runners would stream across the plate.

One such stream sticks in my memory. Monte Kennedy, now gone elsewhere to pitch, was hurling a rare masterpiece one sunny afternoon against the St. Louis Cardinals.

12

He had allowed them just one hit in eight innings, and the Giants led, 1-0. Then, with one out in the ninth, Kennedy started to walk men. This is usually the sign of disaster impending, but somehow Manager Ott decided to stick with his erratic left-hander. And Kennedy promptly struck out a man for the second out.

Then, with the bases loaded, the next man (who should have been the last man to bat in the ball game) hit a little pop fly into short right field, close to the foul line. Back ran Bill Rigney and in ran the right fielder. Then they both stopped, politely, to allow the other free access to the ball. The result of such courtesy was a positive stream of gray and red uniforms, pouring across the plate. My bewildered eye counted three of them. The fourth uniform stopped at third base. But not for long. Enos Slaughter hit a home run for runs four and five.

I do not represent that disaster as unusual. On the contrary, the reason I remember it is that a man sitting next to me in the bleachers shook his head sadly and said, over and over again, "I knew it. I knew it. I knew it." The pop-fly triple was to be expected.

In 1954, however, this bit of business ended abruptly. I do not detract from the Giants and their ability when I say I never saw a luckier team in my life. The law of averages finally swung their way. I now wait in dread for the pendulum to resume its course in the other direction. I expect it will not only swing away from my team, but it will go out of sight for another ten or fifteen years.

Take, for example, one of the few games I saw this past season, a game between the Braves and the Giants at night, the night of September 14, as I recall. For that series Milwaukee brought a badly crippled team into New York. Ed Mathews, their youthful slugger, was not in the lineup. Bob Thomson limped badly, though he was playing. Their regular first baseman, an enormous man named Joe Adcock who had once hit a home run into the center-field bleachers at the Polo Grounds, the only man ever to do so, and who had hit four home runs against the Dodgers in one game in 1954, was missing from the lineup with some injury. A substitute outfielder, George Metkovich, a castoff from the American League, played first base that night. The Milwaukee pitcher was Gene Conley who had recently hurt his back and no one knew whether he was well enough to hurl that night. In fact, even before he threw his first pitch, the Milwaukee management had somebody warming up in the bullpen.

Against this crippled and disorganized team, the Giants fielded their first-string lineup, every man robust, and they had Sal Maglie ready to pitch after a week's rest. On paper (that damnable foolscap) the Giants should have won easily.

So the game went along with Milwaukee taking a 1-0 lead and holding it all the way until the seventh inning. Whitey Lockman, my wife's erstwhile favorite player because she liked his name and his physique—before the days of Willie Mays—Lockman hit a curving fly ball in that seventh inning that headed toward the upper deck in right field. I do not think anybody in the ball park expected the ball to land in fair territory. Lockman, who was in as good a position as any to judge the flight of the ball, stood in the box, knocking the dirt out of his spikes. In every case I have seen previously, the batter always makes some advance toward first base after he has hit the ball. But this time Lockman *knew* the ball was curving foul.

Then, as though the law of averages had made such balls foul for decades and would now start working in the other way, the drive stopped curving. That's the only way I can explain it. It straightened out and hit the foul pole for a home run. The Giants went on to win, 2-1.

14

Once more, I do not minimize the Giants. Having tied the game, they still could have lost it. They didn't.

Or take, for a second example, a ball hit by an opposing batter, Stan Musial, during another night game. This one was hit to deep right-center field and appeared headed for the seats in the grandstand near the three hundred and ninety-five foot marker. Don Mueller, the Giant right fielder, ran to the base of the twelve-foot-high wall and looked up, helpless, as the ball sped merrily toward the seats. But it didn't land in the seats. It took a sudden drop, much as though it had hit an air pocket, and Mueller put out his glove in jerky surprise. The ball landed in the glove.

Of course, those are only two instances, and a season lasts one hundred and fifty-four games, each game full of hundreds of instances. Still, I feel the instances were on the side of the Giants, far, far on their side.

So as this astonishing pennant campaign progressed, through a wonderfully cool summer (that law of averages, again) and on toward the finish, the fans came out of hiding to be on hand for what seemed to be a daily miracle. Pinch hitters, particularly a man named Rhodes, were always hitting home runs when they were most needed; pitchers were pitching shutouts when their team made only a run or two behind them; line drives had "eyes"—that is, Giant-hit balls landed between fielders; the opposition found all the convenient air pockets that led to the waiting glove. And the fans kept coming to see these miracles.

Thus anyone with experience in battling turnstile crowds should have known what the Giant management had known when they moved the gate-opening from ten to nine. I should have known that a great many people would want to be on hand to see this game.

Another mistake was in not appreciating the news that betting was brisk on the series. The big betters, as reported by the same newspapers which usually editorialize against the gambling instinct except where bingo is concerned, were putting their money on the Cleveland Indians, while the small better—the fan, in other words—was wagering on the Giants. In not fully interpreting this latter item— that the baseball fan, like the race track devotee, wants to watch the multiplication or division of his investment—I once more misjudged the enthusiasm that attended this first World Series contest.

Actually, I thought the active betting market stemmed from the "overprice." The odds favoring the Indians were, in the parlance of the trade, eight-nine. That is, if you wished to bet on the Giants, you would get odds of eight to five from your bookie if you are unfortunate enough to have a bookie. This same bookie would demand that you put up nine dollars to his measly five if you wished to bet on Cleveland. Man-to-man (or friend-to-friend, provided one of you is not a bookie), the odds favored the Indians at seventeen to ten.

In any case, a parlay of Rosh Hashana, a desire to see more miracles, and the betting fever should have convinced me that an early crowd would be on hand.

For when I trotted up the Independent stairs and onto 8th Avenue, I could see about a block away a dense crowd gathered around the bleacher entrance. This is the walk, from subway exit to bleacher gate, that I am never quite able to take at a walk. It is here that my emotions break through my artificially leisurely manner. The size of the crowd has nothing to do with it. Even when I know I am in plenty of time, I must run. The sight of the stadium makes me catch my breath. Even the huge sign on this day announcing the first professional football game a month in the offing did not quiet me down.

I started to trot, past the burly policemen, past the early banner and peanut hawkers, past the press gate, and to the bleacher gate. The time was nine-twenty, and as I passed the bleacher entrance, I ducked down low and looked up the ramp that leads to the seating section. What I could see looked crowded.

Well, I thought, my wife was right. I should have brought the non-existent portable radio. I could climb to the top of Coogan's Bluff, overlooking the ball field to the northwest, sit on the rocks and grass, and watch second base while I listened to the game. I had done this many times in my youth. My brother and I would go to the Polo Grounds during the summer recess from school, hoping a boys' club or some social group was getting in free. We'd try to duck into line and sit in the upper left-field stands with a bunch of other boys who did not understand baseball too well and who would clap their hands in unison and yell, "We want a hit," as early as the second inning.

When we failed to get in, which was about half the time, we'd walk up the wooden stairs that lead to the top of Coogan's Bluff on the left-field side of the Polo Grounds. There, with a scattered hundred other fans enjoying a sun bath, we'd "watch" the game. All you can see, through the open-work of the stadium, is the rear portion of the pitcher's mound, the area around second base, and a portion of the outfield. But after a while, you get the hang of it from the noise of the crowd and what the second baseman does.

I remember the first game I saw that way, the Giants against the Phillies. Hubbell was pitching and in a late inning, with the score quite close (the Giants leading, I believe), the Phillies got a man on first with one out. Then on Hubbell's next pitch (you knew the pitch was on its way by the sudden stillness) there was a roar that abruptly broke and then climbed to a shrill scream of delight.

All I could see was the second baseman take one quick

17

step toward the base, then stop and fling his glove behind him to the outfield grass and trot in to the dugout. I'll never forget the elderly Negro sitting next to us in rolled-up white shirtsleeves. He said as he marked his scorecard, "Line drive to Terry. Unassisted double play." He was right.

So I could always climb Coogan's Bluff. Even without my portable radio. Somebody up there would have one.

But—I said to myself—I want to get in. This is a World Series opener. I'd never seen one. There is nothing in baseball to equal it, no, not even the first game of the regular season that means the long winter is over, that means no more foolish incomprehensible mass that is called football, no more whistle-tooting and silly galavanting by ten pituitary freaks that is called basketball, no more dull pushing and stick-jabbing and more whistle-tooting that is called hockey.

No, not even when that first game of the season is—as it was in 1954—the Giants against the Dodgers. No, not even when the Giants win by one run, as they did in 1954. When the season opener is over, you realize, why, that was just one game. Now come the next one hundred and fifty-three.

But the opener of the World Series is different. There is nothing tentative about it; something invariably is proved by it. The speed of a team is established, the strength or weakness of its outfielders' throwing arms, the depth of its bench, and the way the tide of luck is running, all these manifest themselves in that first game between rivals not used to playing each other.

True, the Giants and the Indians had played twenty-one spring-training contests that spring, and for many springs prior, but when one goes back to the newspaper reports of those games, the futility of them as a source of knowledge is dazzlingly clear. What names spring out of those newspaper reports of March 1954? Rudy Regalado, since

18

relegated to pinch-running. Larry Jansen, no longer a Giant pitcher. Jim Hearn, Foster Castleman, Wally Westlake—these are the names that stand out.

And what of the others, the real stars? Well, Antonelli was a disappointment because he had no control and Mike Garcia, more anxious apparently to get in physical shape than to win a game that had no standing, was bombarded steadily by Giant hitters. Mays, of course, was a sensation, but nobody thought much of it because Mays was a .270 hitter who might hit .300, Al Lopez said, if he'd only learn to bunt down the third-base line.

So whatever came out of those training camps and whatever came out of scouting reports would only serve as a tenuous and tentative basis of comparison. What came out of that first game was something else again. Usually, what came out of that first game was the ultimate winner of the entire World Series.

I had my own opinions, of course. Before the first game I had the feeling that the Giants would win, would win handily, not only this game but the entire series. It was not like the time of the 1936 series, when the aging Hubbell had to win that fourth game to even the series and all the time you knew he wouldn't. This was not the Yankees; this was a slow, dull, crippled ball club, the Indians.

So I decided I would take my chances on the line that I should have joined hours earlier and that now stretched away from me, along 8th Avenue and up the western shore of the Harlem River.

The police, about forty strong, were quietly leading the fans to the two double rows of cashiers. The line itself consisted of two parts, the great mass that constituted the major part of the patient waiters, and about a hundred fans at the head of the line who were being allowed to pass through the ticket aisles. The police apparently kept

19

count that way. I do not know that the figure was one hundred, but it looked like one hundred.

The break in the line—between the fortunate few and the hopeful many—was at a little road about a hundred feet from the bleacher entrance. Once you passed that road in your group of a hundred, you seemed sure to get in. That's how I figured it. It seemed a likely way of keeping count, of making sure that not too many people got in and that the fire-department regulations were obeyed in respect to the size of the crowd and its ability to be handled in case of fire, panic or other possibilities that seem in the realm of improbability.

So I walked to the end of the line, about a quarter of a mile away, counting off each group of approximately a hundred fans. I wanted to know what my chances would be. By the time I reached the end of the line, I had checked off exactly thirty such masses. If my arithmetic and eye were sound, there were three thousand people in front of me. The only problem remaining was how many people had already gone in.

I moved into line. The line was actually not a line but a waving mass three and four not quite abreast. There are three-thousand-nine-hundred bleacher seats at the Polo Grounds, although how this number has ever been arrived at is beyond me. The bleacher seats are not seats at all, but long narrow wooden planks. Probably the figure was set by the number of tickets sold on a day that all the plank space was taken up.

The Giant management had also announced that in addition to these bleacher seats four thousand standing-room tickets would be put on sale at the same time, though no line for those was visible when I started my vigil.

So—despite the three thousand people in front of me —I did not feel too let down. I should have been here hours earlier, but here I was anyway, and it would have to do. If I could not get into the bleachers, I would buy a standing-room ticket and squat behind the reserved-seat section in the lower grandstand. The bleacher seat would cost two dollars and ten cents; the standing-room ticket four dollars and twenty cents.

However, after a wait of two or three minutes, the line moved as more fans (my estimated hundred at a clip) went through the gates, and we approached that little road-way which served to distinguish the immediately fortunate from the potentially so. The line continued moving every few minutes. I looked at my watch, and it was now nine-forty. I had been on line twenty minutes.

Then I did some more swift and highly doubtful arith-metic. If the gates had indeed opened at nine, then twenty minutes of people going through those gates had already occurred by the time I got on line. Another twenty minutes had gone by since. The same number of people, approx-imately, should have gone in during each twenty-minute period.

I studied the line ahead of me. It seemed that I was about halfway toward the gates; that is, I had moved about the same distance on the line as I had remaining in front of me. Fifteen hundred people was half the line (all depending on my original guess as to the look of a hundred people on such a line); they had gone in while I waited. If the gates had opened at nine and people moved at the same speed then as now, fifteen hundred other people were in-side when I got on line. That meant three thousand already inside, and about fifteen hundred more standing in front of me. Four thousand, five hundred people, and then me.

I hoped my arithmetic was wrong in some manner; I further hoped that the police department didn't know how big the bleachers were, that they confused the Polo

21

Grounds with the larger Yankee Stadium, across the river. I hoped in case my arithmetic was right that the Giant management wanted my two dollars and ten cents so badly it would wink at fire-department restrictions. I just plain hoped.

I had made the acquaintance of a gentleman who said he had motored up on his fall vacation some seven hundred miles to see the game.

"From Cleveland?" I said, not knowing the distance between the two cities.

"No," he said, "from North Carolina." He mentioned a small town, the name of which eludes me now.

I was relieved. I did not want to sit next to somebody from Cleveland. I did not want to hear disparaging remarks about the old Polo Grounds and its nearby foul lines, its blind spots, its tiny, cramped bleachers. I felt it would be expected that I play the host, put a mild restraint on my enthusiasm, lean over backwards and murmur, "Bully," every time an Indian distinguished himself.

But he was not a Cleveland fan. Also, he revealed himself as a cousin of Max Lanier, former Giant pitcher and before that a member of the St. Louis Cardinals during three pennant years. Lanier, as I recalled, "jumped" to the Mexican League. My informant told me that Cousin Max had just finished a year with Beaumont in the Texas League and would retire from baseball soon. I am always concerned when a baseball player's career is finished because, for the most part, ball players can do nothing except play ball.

Lately, of course, they have developed a knowledge of the saloon or liquor-store business, but I feel this is a fad that will soon be worn thin. Barflies are particular people and strange people. They seem to patronize a certain saloon regardless, more interested in what's in their glass

22

than in who was responsible for putting it there. And the people who stray into Baseball Joe's bar because they rooted hard for Joe during his career are transient drinkers. As the years pass, the glory of Baseball Joe fades. More vital is the temperature of his beer, the pleasantness of his bartender, and the fullness of his measure.

So I expressed my concern about Cousin Max. The man from North Carolina assured me there was no need to worry about Lanier. The three World Series shares, his bonus for signing to play in the Mexican League, and his salaries up here and down there had made any more baseball just a passing hobby with Lanier.

"How big was that bonus?" I asked. I had heard about the fabulous monies paid by the Mexican League heads to lure major leaguers south of the border, but I always held those figures suspect.

"Fifty thousand," he said.

"And what did they pay him down there?"

"Twenty-seven thousand a year."

So I stopped worrying.

Then my new friend told me a bit more about his home town, how Al Rosen had played Class D ball down there for a manager that Rosen said was the best he had ever played for.

"Is he still managing down there?" I asked.

"No," he said. "Some major-league team—the Braves, I think—signed him up as a scout."

It made me feel good. Usually those little anecdotes end up so dismally. I was sure that this nameless manager would still be down there in that little town whose name I cannot recall, playing out his days before a few hundred people every game. Many a rose, I thought, is born to blush unseen, and many a rose is not.

I said, "Do you think we'll get in?"

He said, "Depends."

I am in awe of out-of-towners. I somehow link the still-water-runs-deep adage to their laconic ways. On reflection, I am glad I did not ask the next question, "Depends on what?" He might have said, in his drawl, "On whether they got room for us or not." Still, such a question would deserve such an answer.

We then discussed the series and he agreed that the Giants would probably win, though he expected the series to run longer than I did. It seemed to me that the Giants would win in either four or five games,*depending on whether they could beat Early Wynn in the second contest. I felt that Wynn, off his late season record, was the best pitcher on either club, and I had been mildly surprised when Cleveland manager Al Lopez had announced Bob Lemon as his first game starter. Still, I am not an American League fan; all I know about the Indians is what I have read about them in the papers.

But I felt—and my friend agreed—that the Indians, hobbled by injuries, did not appear to be anywhere near as puissant as their one hundred and eleven victories in pennant play would signify. Though the Giants had won far fewer games, they had beaten every team in the National League more often than any team had beaten them. On the other hand, while the Indians feasted on the teams from fourth place down, they had lost to as often as they had won from the Yankees and the Chicago White Sox.

While we were thus talking, a young man with a heavy Spanish accent said, "You bet. Indians couldn't even beat Cardinals." Somebody said something that sounded like, "Nnahhh," and the young man said excitedly, "You see. You see." Then the line moved and everybody shut up.

On one side of the line was the street and, beyond it,

* No, I did not bet on the series.

the river bank. On the other side, the inside, was the beginning of an apartment house project. At that moment, a boy standing on the grass of the housing project walked over to the line and said, "You'll never get in. The place is filled." Then he started to walk away.

I yelled, "Is it?" and he turned and grinned and shrugged. I said again, "Is it?" and he walked away.

My North Carolina friend said, "Boy's just joshing us."

I thought my friend was indulging in wishful thinking and I felt sorry for him. I said, "I'll tell you what. If through some fluke, I'm the last one to get in, you can have my place in line." He had joined the line right after me, so by all rights I was ahead, though we walked abreast.

A coffee hawker came up and said, "Big cuppa coffee."

My friend bought a cup, a small cup it was. "How much?" he said.

"Fifteen cents," the man said.

I was amazed. True, it was a small cup, but on World Series days when the audience is a captive one, at the mercy of the monopolistic entrepreneur, I expected the coffee vendor would get twenty-five cents for his product. It was a chilly morning and the people on line were paying approximately three hundred percent of the usual price for a bleacher seat.

I do not like weak, sweetish coffee in cardboard cups so I did not buy a cup. But I hoped many people would.

While my friend drank his coffee, we walked along, and suddenly it became a fact that the boy had been joshing or else guessing. We reached and crossed the little roadway, and now there were a hundred-or-so of us quickly divided into two clearcut lines, shuffling toward the cashiers. My little act of courtesy was wasted, I saw. My friend got on the line on the right and I on the left. His moved faster and he disappeared inside. It was the last I saw of him.

THREE

I bought my bleacher seat, number 1662, gave it to the ticket-taker who tore it in half and handed me my raincheck. I went up the ramp. At the head of the ramp, a young man in familiar white uniform was selling what he called souvenir programs. All I wanted was the old-fashioned everyday kind of program with a scorecard, the kind that sells for a dime, but he didn't have any of those. So I purchased a souvenir program for fifty cents and went up the stone steps in the left-center-field bleacher section.

There are two bleacher sections to the Polo Grounds, one to the left-field side and the other to the right-field side of the deepest center field. About a hundred feet up, the two sections join and rise another hundred feet or so to accommodate the three thousand, nine hundred plank dwellers. A runway extends from the playing field in deep center field to the exit gates and serves to split the two bleacher sections.

It is invariably wiser to go over to the right-center-field

section because it fills up later. The only entrance to the bleachers is on the left-center-field side and although this is the "visiting" team side (the visiting dugout, the visiting bullpen, and the visiting clubhouse are all on the left-field side at the Polo Grounds), it is where most people choose to sit. I, too, like to sit there.

When the Giants are using a right-handed pitcher (as they were today), I prefer sitting slightly left of center. This places me on a line with the pitcher's right hand as it delivers the pitch and home plate. Despite the better than five hundred feet distance, I can easily follow the ball when I sit this way and after an inning or two no longer have to wait for the umpire's sign or look at the scoreboard to tell balls from strikes. Once in a while I'm mistaken, but then, I remind myself, umpires are human.

It was now ten o'clock according to the big clock at the top of the bleachers. The entire left-center-field section seemed filled. But since these are not seats, I did not lose heart immediately. I looked for some space between two people. Usually six inches is enough as a starter. There were many such spaces. They were, however, "reserved." A seat is reserved by the presence of a newspaper or a hat or some small indication that the party sitting there will be right back. It is seldom that these little signs are ignored. Bleacher fans for all their vociferousness are a comradely bunch—at least until the game begins.

About halfway up, just when I was about to give up this side and scoot over to the right-field seats, I saw two men in sports jackets playing cards. The space for the cards was more than the space I would need. Naturally I did not want to break up their game. But I did want a seat. So I asked one of the players, a rail-thin middle-aged man who was building fours in a casino game (he used the term "stacking") whether anyone else was using that space. He said no, and I squeezed in on the kibitzer's side of the game, still leaving enough room for the game to go on.

I watched them play for a minute or so until my neighbor failed to pick up the two of spades, an ace and the three of hearts on the board with the six of hearts in his hand. He contented himself with picking up the two with a two from his hand. I looked over from time to time but the quality of the game did not improve. Still, my neighbor won. I felt this was some sort of omen. I was rooting for him, in an offhand way, and he won. Good, I thought.

I had brought a *New York Times* with me and I tried to read the paper slowly. I spent nearly a half hour on the crossword puzzle because the upper left hand corner eluded me until I realized that the baseball team was the Orioles and the meaning of "way up" was "stair." I had foolishly thought "way" was an adverb, and I worked on "in air," or "on air," for several minutes. However, all went down and correctly, I think, and I still had nearly two and a half hours to wait before the game would start. So I turned to my souvenir program.

I read the notes on all the players, spending most of my attention on the Indians. I studied all the pictures and found two more good omens there. The pictures of the Indians had been retouched. All the backgrounds had been airbrushed out, or else the pictures had been taken in a portrait studio with a fake blank background used, whereas most of the Giants were pictured with the ball field behind them. That was good; ball players belonged on a ball field, not in a photographer's studio. I felt the Indians were a soft and pampered crew. Secondly, the Giants seemed much grimmer a lot. And rightly, I thought. This was no tea party, I chided the smiling Indians. Look at Dark, I told them. He's positively ugly. And Maglie, sneering; Henry Thompson with his nose wrinkled as though scent-

Sal Maglie, right-handed pitcher

ing the prey. Why, man, I said to Al Rosen who looked as though he were a movie idol, this is *baseball*.

Fifteen more minutes went by in this manner.

Then I took out my feelings on the people who had made the programs. The usual ten-cent scorecard has the probable lineup already printed in. Not so on this one. Since there was little doubt as to the two starting lineups with the exception of whether Monte Irvin or Dusty Rhodes would play left field and who would pitch, the blank lineup was a stupid bother. It meant I would have to print in the eighteen names, numbers and positions, and my printing is barely legible.

A few minutes before eleven o'clock, Sal Maglie, impeccably dressed in a tan sports jacket and dark slacks, walked from the exit gate in right field across the outfield to the Giant dressing-room steps. He was greeted by the bleacher fans who do not need to see a ball player in uniform and then have to wait until he turns and reveals his number to know who he is. Maglie had a rather sheepish grin on his face as though he were sorry so many people had had to get up so early. Or it may be that he was embarrassed by his very clean, close shave.

Maglie is best known to the fans and to opposing batsmen by his thick black beard and a remarkable scowl that he achieves by pulling down the corners of his mouth. On the mound he acts as though he hates every batter in the world, and it is possible that he does. Maglie, at the start of the series play, was over thirty-seven years old, a man with a lame back and a vanished fast ball. All he has now is his wonderful curve ball, his control and what appears to be a tremendous desire to win.

With these three assets, Maglie clings to the major leagues after a distressingly mediocre record in the minors. Now, near the end of his career, it must be a bleak and

30

bitter thing to know that his talent and the recognition of it came so late, and that he has so little time left in which to use it. Glancing over the Giant roster, one notes Paul Giel, born fifteen years after Maglie. Giel received a bonus of $60,000 to sign with the Giants in 1954, fresh from his university campus. And racing down the roster reveals only one other ball player on the entire squad born before the '20's.

So Maglie must sense the desperation of it all, the attempt to cram into five or six seasons what other men spread out over twelve or fifteen. And there is only one man who has kept Maglie from getting to the major leagues earlier, only one man who has kept him from winning more often: the man with the bat. No wonder, then, the black scowl, the flaming hate.

But when he is not pitching, Maglie appears the most affable of men. Giant fans warm up slowly to new members of their team. Maglie, with his beard and fierce countenance and his faculty for throwing swift pitches straight at a man's temple, did not receive a friendly reception in the beginning of his Giant career. But now the spectators realize his ability stems from just such pitches: first, the fast ball inside, then the curve or change-of-pace pitch on the outside corner. The great and even more hated Jackie Robinson says Maglie is so good because, "he keeps moving the ball."

And the fans now seem to look forward to Maglie and his methods. As he walked slowly across the outfield, the green grass still dew dotted and shining in the hazy sunlight, a cool breeze in the autumn air, the fans yelled friendly words to him. He waved back half-heartedly, still smiling sheepishly, and a man two rows in front of me yelled, "Stick it in their ears today, Sal."

Here is the friendly sadism, the vicarious barbarism that

31

makes a baseball spectator a fanatic. It is an element of baseball that annoys my wife. When I mouth such sentiments as, "Stick it in their ears," or encourage a Giant runner to "chop his leg off," as he sets off for the next base, my wife stares at me and shakes her head. She just does not understand that none of this must be taken literally.

I am sickened when a man is hit by a pitched baseball. I'll never forget the sight—and the sound—of a pitch thrown by Bucky Walters hitting Billy Jurges over the left ear. Jurges dropped like a felled oak, and for a brief second, the game stopped as though this scene must forever be ingrained. No one moved. Walters had finished his follow through, right hand in front of his left knee, body bent forward. The catcher, half-risen from his crouch, stared at the fallen figure. The infield froze while the echo of crunch reverberated through the hushed stands.

Fans do not enjoy such scenes. They are not bullfight *aficionados,* waiting wet-lipped for the gore, either the bull's or the matador's. But they *are* exponents of the exaggeration as a means of communication. "Hit it a mile, Willie," someone will shout to Mays even though he knows no man has ever hit a ball within four thousand, six hundred feet of a mile. And so a man shouts to Maglie, without fear of contradiction, "Stick it in their ears today, Sal."

But not all the fans were on Maglie's side. As he mounted the stairs a woman in a red beret to my right and about five rows down shouted that he'd be getting an early shower. I leaped into the fray and announced to all and sundry that she was an American-League bum.

She stood up, turned around and faced me. "Who says I'm an American-League bum?" she yelled.

I said, "I say so. You're an American-League bum."

She held up a banner and waved it at me. It read "Brooklyn Dodgers."

That seemed to satisfy both of us. We sat down.

A few minutes later the Giants started trooping down the stairs in their white uniforms with orange trimming, and there was more friendly applause dotted with an occasional hostile remark. On the whole, however, it was a quiet, well-behaved crowd. It seemed that the Giant fans held no deep animosity for the Indians. They did not hate them, for instance, the way they hated the Dodgers or the Yankees. The next day the newspapers reported that there were many Indian partisans present, but it is more likely that these were Giant fans greeting the visitors with pleasant cordiality and curiosity.

Giant fans are unique. I have never seen anything like them, in any sport. They certainly differ vastly from their city rivals, the Yankee or the Dodger supporters. A Yankee fan is a complacent ignorant fat cat. He knows nothing about baseball except that the Yankees will win the pennant and World Series more often than they won't and that a home run is the only gesture of any worth in the entire game. They have been fed on victory and on great dull stars such as Lou Gehrig, Joe DiMaggio and Mickey Mantle, and even these men they do not appreciate. They know that DiMaggio could hit the ball often and for great distances and that he could make marvelous plays in the outfield, but they never knew that he was one of the very best baserunners in the American League.

I remember seeing DiMaggio hit a ground ball past the shortstop in an unimportant game one afternoon several years back. As the ball rolled into left-center field, the two outfielders converged on it. DiMaggio rounded first and as I glanced at him, something caught in my throat. He looked more like a great deer than a human, running lightly on his toes, head and neck stretched out, nostrils seemingly quivering, eyes searching for whatever it was he had to know. And then when the center fielder decided it was to be his play rather than the left fielder's, a routine play of gathering up the ball and returning it to the infield, DiMaggio made his move. He dashed—no, strode is the better word—he strode for second, long-legged and sure, and the center fielder, in a sudden flurry of activity, a man upset because the unconventional was being done, threw in a hurry to second base, but a scant fraction of a second too late.

It was not a game-winning effort in itself—the Yankees won, 9-1—but it was symbolic of the skill of Yankee players of that time. DiMaggio had hit an ordinary single. But because it was so ordinary, the left fielder—the man moving in on the ball and toward second base at the same time —did not make the play that he should have made, and the center fielder had to cut in front of him, moving *away* from second base as he picked up the ball. It was just this very thing that DiMaggio sensed might happen, and he was prepared to act if it did.

But the remarkable thing is that nobody cheered. Nobody. Not a single soul in the entire ball park. Oh, yes, they cheered the blow. As soon as the ball was hit they yelled, and when it rolled past the shortstop they increased the yell for now it was surely a hit. But by the time the outfielder picked up the ball, they were silent, absolutely dead silent. It was a display of mass ignorance that I have never seen equaled in a ball park. I have never gone back to the Yankee Stadium since that day.

Dodger fans are not ignorant at all. They would have appreciated DiMaggio's daring move but it would remain unacknowledged except in their tinny souls. Dodger fans are a surly lot, riddled by secret fears and inferiority complexes which have good basis, of course. They have suffered with not only inferior teams in the past, but also with the specter of clowns in uniform instead of baseball players. The sight of two Dodger runners on one base is legend. That this happens as often to other ball teams is ignored. It seems a Dodger trademark, and the fans know it. It is a stigma and not even pennant-winning teams can remove it. Thus, they take their secret shame with them wherever they go, and to compensate they become rude, overbearing and superlative-addicted.

No one—they say, and they usually say it in the manner of John L. Sullivan announcing he can lick any s.o.b. in the house—no one ever threw as well as Carl Furillo. Now Furillo is a wonderful thrower, one of the finest. But to hear the Dodger fans speak, there never was a Bob Meusel or a Myril Hoag or a Terry Moore or an Eddie Roush. To say nothing of Willie Mays.

No one—they say—ever swung as smoothly as Duke Snider. (This they usually say right after Snider has struck out; compensation, once more.) Snider is admittedly a picture of beauty and grace and strength at the plate. And yet has there ever been a swing like Ruth's?

They tell you that Gilliam is a better ball player than Davey Williams even though he cannot pivot on the double play, requisite reflex with a second baseman.

I say all this with the prejudiced eye of a Giant fan, and I know it is the truth.

Still, I would take a Yankee fan or a Dodger over the fans of any other city.

In Pittsburgh, I heard the fans boo a rival pitcher because of his habit of throwing to first base when a swift Pirate baserunner took his short dancing lead. I do not mind that they are against the rival pitcher and for their own baserunner. That's good. But I mind their ignorance.

They do not understand that a man on base *must* make his move for second on an attempted steal *before* the pitcher makes his final decision to throw to the plate. If the runner waits that split second too long—or until the pitcher is firmly committed to throw to the batter and cannot now change his move without a balk being called —the runner will not make second base safely provided the rival team does not err defensively.

The pitcher has his weapon, his throw to first. If he catches the runner "on the wrong leg"—that is, with his weight already thrown forward, toward second base—the runner will probably be picked off base.

The runner has his weapon: timing. More than daring or speed, perfect timing is the trick to stealing bases. Thus, one of the beauties of baseball unfolds while the runner takes his lead and the pitcher throws to first: it is a battle between two individual opponents within the fabric of the greater mass struggle.

I do not boo such a maneuver. I sit enthralled by it. It is baseball.

In Milwaukee, I have heard the fans cheer every foul ball hit by their home-team batters. In the beginning it must be thrilling to the players to know that there is such undeviating partisanship, such blind loyalty behind them. But after a while, they must wonder whether every day isn't Ladies' Day.

I do not mind overwhelming loyalty. I concede to no man in the matter of loyalty. I understand it. My favorite baseball radio announcer was a man named Fred Hoey who broadcast Boston games over station WICC which I believe is a Bridgeport station. He used to break the unwritten rule of baseball announcers; he took definite sides in his broadcast. I remember a time that the Braves were at bat in a late inning with the Giants, the score tied, and Urbanski—I forget his first name—at the plate. There were two out, and Rabbit Maranville was on second base. I think the pitcher for the Giants was Fitzsimmons.

On Fitzsimmons' pitch, Hoey announced in the approved fashion, though his eagerness was apparent in his voice, "There's a line drive to left field. It's a hit." And then, unable to stand by a neutral party, Hoey would stop broadcasting and start urging hoarsely, while you could hear his fists pounding the ledge in front of him, "Come on, Rabbit, come on, Rabbit!" Then a deadly pause while Hoey regained his official composure and finally, "Maranville is out at the plate, Moore to Mancuso."

Hoey was a radio announcer and a good one. He also was a fiercely loyal man. I admired him.

But in Milwaukee it is stupid loyalty, dull and tiresome, this screeching over every pop fly hit by a Brave batter.

Philadelphia is worse. In the City of Brotherly Love, I have been shocked by the anti-Negro, anti-Semitic remarks made by the fans, not just a few of them, but many.

In other cities, the fandom is notoriously ignorant, unfair, or surly—sometimes all three. Only in the Polo Grounds do you get a solid mass of intelligent, polite, yet loyal spectators. Perhaps because they love baseball even more than they do the Giants.

And so when the Indians started finally to troop down their dressing-room steps to the outer edges of the field, the bleacher fans yelled mild greetings or else watched them intently, measuring the girth of their backs, trying to see how badly Al Rosen was limping, studying Larry Doby as he kept hunching and relaxing his shoulders as though the muscles up there, under the gray and blue uniform, were sore. This was the enemy, for the most part unknown, and it had to be reconnoitered.

The most popular Indian seemed to be Mike Garcia, the

third member of Cleveland's renowned pitching trio, of which Lemon and Wynn are the first two. Garcia is an enormous, dark-complexioned man who looks strong enough to squeeze juice out of baseballs. When someone from the bleachers called his name, he turned around and waved, grinning broadly.

Then he joined a few of his teammates in running across the outfield, from left to right, and walking back. The sprints appeared to be competitive races. If they were, then Garcia is an astonishingly fast man for one so large. The program lists him as six feet one inch and two hundred pounds, but he must be two inches taller and thirty pounds heavier than that, which is why the fans call him the Big Bear. In his practice dashes, he was outdistancing his lighter and swifter-looking mates. Of course, it may have been not so much Garcia's speed as the others' lack of it.

The batting practice started at eleven-fifteen when there were the few thousand bleacher fans and about the same number of scattered grandstand onlookers. The Giant substitutes took first turns. Joe Amalfitano, number twelve (I had to look at the program to identify him), was the first man to bat and he fouled off the first pitch. He was to take more swings than any other Giant. Every time there was a lull in the proceedings, he would run around the batting cage and take his stance for one more swing.

Amalfitano is a man who achieved peculiar fame in a game late in the regular season. Before that game, this bonus rookie had been in a handful of games as a substitute runner. He had never batted or fielded in a major-league contest. The World Series program wryly notes on Amalfitano: "Appeared only infrequently in the Giant lineup this year, but made himself useful and highly popular with the team with his earnest willingness to perform all the handyman chores. . . ."

I pictured young Amalfitano tying other people's shoe-laces and rubbing the gloss from baseballs, busily opening beer bottles and applying liniment to somebody else's sore muscle. I wondered what would happen to such a handy fellow when and if baseball ever became union organized.

But one sweltering day in July, after manager Durocher had used all his other infielders in some capacity or other out in Cincinnati, it became incumbent that the handyman drop his mop and pick up a fielder's glove. Amalfitano is apparently a third baseman, judging from his station in infield practice, but on this day, with the thermometer registering 105 degrees, he played two positions, even though he had never officially played in the field before.

Durocher had to make a choice here. He had Hank Thompson and Amalfitano in the infield at the same time. Thompson is the regular Giant third baseman, though he can play second in a pinch, provided the pinch does not insist that he pivot on a double play. Nobody, not even Junior Gilliam, pivots worse than Thompson.

One of the two young men—Thompson or the untried Amalfitano—would have to play second, while the other played third. Durocher gazed into his crystal ball; Amalfitano went to third. The problem, of course, in this steaming arena and with the Giants protecting a one-run lead, was how to keep the ball away from Amalfitano. Here the fantastic luck (and intuition) that linked themselves with the Giants all season came to the fore. A tricky ground ball went down to second, where Thompson handled it competently.

Then Durocher paused for another look into the crystal ball (and at the Cincinnati hitter, a man named Andy Seminick who likes to pull the ball down the third-base line). Durocher called time; Amalfitano and Thompson shifted positions. And Seminick hit the ball viciously down to third

39

where Thompson again fielded it competently, and for the final out of the game.

Amalfitano had come through unscathed, and unsullied by any contact with a batted ball.

During the last five days of the regular season, after the Giants had clinched the pennant, Amalfitano did play on occasion and he acquitted himself handily.

Still, he had batted fewer than ten times during the regular season and he would surely bat not at all in the series. Yet he took at least thirty swings during that first day's batting practice.

It has been a superstition of mine that the team hitting fewer balls into the stands during batting practice will go on to win that ball game. It is as though the other team has squandered all its power before it counted. The Giants now certainly made me feel that my earlier hopes and prediction of victory would bear fruit. Man after man swung and missed or fouled the ball.

After a while, I stopped expecting to see every other pitch hit into the stands. I started hoping the ball would at least reach the outfield. Only Dusty Rhodes was hitting with any authority, and this meant little because I was sure the Giant manager, Leo Durocher, would start Monte Irvin and keep Rhodes on the bench until his batting skill was required. This would give the Giants defensive strength in left field and pinchhitting power when it could best be used.

The futility at the plate became intriguing and I started studying the pitcher to discover what he was throwing up there. The pitcher was Alex Konikowski, a young man with a fairly good fast ball, but certainly not one of the hurlers who is more mysterious to the hitters. During the regular season, in fact, Konikowski's pitches seemed to have an affinity for rival bats and he had thus been sparingly used all year. He was employed only when a game seemed beyond even the Giants' miraculous reach or else when the rest of the pitching staff had been used up the day before.

I saw Konikowski in just one game. That was against St. Louis. He made his appearance after the Giants trailed by seven runs or maybe it was only five. He pitched with some stubborn skill for a while, but when the Cardinal second baseman, Al Schoendienst, hit a foul smash deep into the upper deck in right field, Konikowski seemed to wilt. It looked almost as though he knew he couldn't get Schoendienst out. So he threw the pitch most hurlers reserve for the three-ball-and-no-strike situation when the batter is not likely to swing.

Schoendienst swung.

Today, however, Konikowski appeared to be the greatest pitcher in the world. Yet on closer scrutiny, all he was throwing were straight pitches, swift enough but not overpowering, and coming in about chest high over the middle of the plate.

After a while he was replaced by a man named Al Worthington. Ah, I thought, now we'll see some action. Worthington pitched two shutouts in his first two major league starts, but after that it seemed he could hardly get a man out.

Well, on this day, he pitched his third shutout. He is a bit faster than Konikowski, which is pretty fast, but he evidently understood his intended role. He was just throwing the ball somewhat in the manner of a man warming up to pitch, rather than bearing down. By the time he and the Giants had finished I counted forty swinging strikes.

Nevertheless I was beginning to have my first niggling doubts about victory. I had hoped the Giants wouldn't hit the ball too well in practice, but I hadn't wanted them to look downright futile. Then I recalled with further misgiving that in the last game with Brooklyn in the last week of the season, they had been shut out by a rookie left hander named Spooner who had struck out fifteen of them. And in the final series of the season, the Giants had not been attacking the Philadelphia pitchers, their favorite cousins, with their customary vigor. So I sadly concluded that my champions were in a serious batting slump.

A few minutes later, my hopes perked considerably. If the Giants couldn't hit in their licks, neither could the Indians. Only Larry Doby, the strong center fielder who takes a frightening swing at the ball, much like Duke Snider, was putting drives into the stands with any regularity. And he was doing it with some of the most awesome shots I had ever seen. They were hit along the foul line, which boded ill for the Giants since the right-field fence at the foul line is only two hundred and fifty-seven feet from the plate, the shortest distance in either league necessary for a home run. The balls Doby hit went streaking on a rising line, several of them bouncing off the façade over the second tier just below the roof. A couple went over the roof and disappeared.

This activity on Doby's part was a source of delight to the woman in the red beret who sat to my right and below. She kept bouncing up and down every time Doby connected, and shouted, "Attaboy, Larry, attaboy. You show him, Larry boy."

I countered with a derisive shout, "Two o'clock hitter, Doby. That's all you are."

It is possible that some of my young readers do not understand such a retort. People in the bleachers do. In the old days when games were played swiftly, the starting time was three-fifteen in the afternoon. This, despite the fact that there were no lights to turn on when it became the least bit dim. Batting practice occurred around two.

42

So a two o'clock hitter was a man who kept hitting practice balls into the stands, but who during the game failed to do any damage.

After Doby finished his licks, and the next man started swinging and missing, I turned my attention to the Indian players stationed all over the outfield.

I said to the man on my right, not the casino player, "Where's Feller? I haven't seen him all day."

He looked up and pointed. "There," he said, "doing pushups."

Over in right-center field, Bob Feller was indeed doing pushups, palms flat on the ground as his arms pushed his body up and down. They were not very good pushups because Feller hinged a bit at the hips, shoving his posterior too high so that his body never was flat in either the up or down position.

Then suddenly I felt quite saddened. Feller, now thirty-five years old, one of the really good pitchers of the last twenty years, carefully and not too well doing calisthenics in the outfield, keeping himself in shape for a pitching call he must have felt wouldn't come unless things became terribly desperate for his club. Feller, who at seventeen years of age could throw a ball so fast the eye could scarcely follow it, and who could do so with two days' rest between games, now a once-a-week pitcher, usually reserved for the weaker hitting teams of which the American League has so many.

I had seen Feller pitch in an All-Star game at the Yankee Stadium in, I think, 1939. He had entered the game with runners on base after the pitcher—Tommy Bridges, I believe—had started to weaken, and with his first pitch Feller induced Arky Vaughan to hit into a double play to end the inning. After that, he really warmed to his task. He threw three pitches to Johnny Mize, probably then the

43

best hitter in his league, which not even Mize—who had great vision—could have seen too well. They were a slender blur of white, those pitches, pouring like cream past Mize, and it is a tribute to the great slugger that he swung at more or less the same time the ball passed him. Of course, he didn't hit any of the pitches, not even a thin foul.

Feller did the same to Dolf Camilli and Camilli also swung and also missed, three times. Those six pitches, thrown by a man who was still too young to vote, must have been as fast as any ever thrown by anyone.

Feller won't remember me, but I once met him, at a re-ception–press conference–cocktail party early in 1948. I was distressed to see the nervous tic that worried his mouth and eye. He seemed to be a man driving himself too hard, knowing even then what Maglie knows today, that time is the real enemy, even more than the man with the bat. And I thought to myself on that afternoon: He's through.

That was six and a half years ago, and here he was in another World Series, diligently pushing his tired body up and down, trying to keep the fading muscles strong and loose for the call that probably wouldn't come.

Then the cage at home plate was rolled away, and the teams traded places, the Giants coming out for their field-ing practice. The Giant outfielders went to their posts and I watched closely because fielding practice today is a thing rushed through almost before it has begun. Monte Irvin and Dusty Rhodes in left field were the first on display. Each was hit four balls, two of which were thrown to home plate and two to second base. I made it a contest and though I expected Irvin to far surpass his admittedly weak-throwing teammate, it had to be scored a standoff. Irvin threw harder and further, but on this occasion Rhodes threw more accurately. However, he was pampered a bit, I thought. The balls he fielded were not hit hard, so he

44

could take them coming in on the run and therefore quite close to the infield.

In center field, by himself, was Willie Mays, number twenty-four facing the bleacher fans. Mays is my wife's current favorite, and I strongly suspect he will so remain for another fifteen years. Mays is, to my mind, the finest ball player the National League has employed since Eddie Roush. He was, in his first full season of play, a better ball player already than Terry Moore in his prime, even in the field. Because of his astonishing ability to get rid of the ball quickly, he seems a better center fielder than Joe Di-Maggio, who threw on a lower trajectory but who did not possess the speed of foot or hand that are Mays'.

Mays made his first throw into third base without a bounce, the ball arriving at the third baseman's glove about two inches to the left, or second-base side, of third. It was a magnificent throw but one wondered whether it would have done any good in a game, since the third baseman, anchored of necessity near his bag so that he can make a tag, prefers his throws from center field to be slightly on the outfield side of third, rather than the infield. This way there is less likelihood of a baserunner's spikes displacing the ball before it reaches the third baseman's glove.

Apparently Mays realized this error. His second throw took the outer edge of the bag on the fly. Mays thereupon devoted his interests to home plate. He threw his first practice ball to the catcher without a bounce, the ball arriving about waist high, directly over the plate. Once more he improved the second time around. His last throw came in slightly lower the whole way and was gathered in by the catcher ankle high, the tip of the catcher's glove resting on home plate.

I do not believe I ever saw a more impressive display in my baseball life, and I have watched baseball intently for twenty-eight years. I remember the uncanny accuracy of Joe Moore when he played left field for the Giants, and how, during fielding practice, a man would stand at home plate with a bat while Moore fired the ball to the catcher. As often as not the ball passed over the strike zone.

But that was a show. Moore took his time and the batter undoubtedly helped give him a better target. And, as I say, often as not, his throws split the plate. The other half didn't, and sometimes they were badly off. Still, Moore was a very fine thrower. He wasn't a Mays, however. On this early afternoon, Mays did not seem to be Mays either. He appeared superhuman.

The few hundred fans who were watching Mays gave him a spattering of applause. The woman in the red hat was talking to her neighbor. I felt sorry for her.

That is the sad part of fielding practice. It is mostly ignored today. In the old days (this probably sounds a bit presumptuous to those who were already veterans of many campaigns when I saw my first game in 1926), in those days I remember the Giant infield of Terry, Critz, Jackson and Lindstrom, the "million-dollar infield" as it was called, and it used to perform up to its name in fielding practice. They were so deft, so quick, so breathtaking that the fans would sit, first in stunned silence, and then in gathering bedlam to roar as each man made his play and the ball sped at dizzying speed about the infield. But that was 1930. To-day, fielding practice seems to be a waste of time. The substitutes clutter up the premises and the regulars merely go through the motions. Only a man like Mays makes it a work of art. After he had finished, the ball was hit to Don Mueller, a journeyman outfielder, and I stopped watching.

I had a new interest. Sal Maglie was warming up in the right-field bullpen, the home-team site used by relief pitchers, and another reason why I chose to sit in the left-field section of the bleachers. I could see the Giant bullpen and I would know by the activity out there how worried Manager Durocher was. I did not care too keenly about the goings-on in the Indian bullpen, the corner of which I could barely see. Just so long as the Giants were scoring, I cared not a whit who was pitching or preparing to pitch against them.

It was surprising to see Maglie in the bullpen. Usually the Giant pitcher warms up in front of the Giant dugout, between home plate and first base. Maglie probably thought the opening-game festivities, which sometimes includes parades, speeches, comedy acts, "first-ball" throwings and other sundries of no appeal to baseball fans, might disturb his practicing.

Maglie with a baseball in his hand is a different man from the Maglie in sports jacket, wearing a sheepish grin. Now his face was grim. He was laboring the ball to the plate in the ungraceful manner that is his. He looks as though each pitch hurts someplace, and for all any of us know, it may. Maglie pitched the game that clinched the pennant in 1954, a night contest with the Dodgers, a team he has beaten so often as to take on legendary aspects. While batting early in the game, Maglie swung viciously at a pitch and missed. Immediately he clutched his back, his face screwed up in surprised pain. Three minutes later he was back at the plate, giving no evidence of any ache. But after the game, during the wild pennant-winning celebration, one of the Giant radio announcers asked Maglie if his back bothered him at all after he had hurt it while batting. Maglie stopped being affable immediately. He snapped, "Suppose we forget about that, huh?"

It is *his* back, and, if it exists, *his* pain. He is the one who must carry it through his last few years as an active,

47

first-line pitcher. His snarling silence is like Feller's push-ups; both belie the flagging strength and, unfortunately, at the same time point attention to it.

But though I was surprised to find Maglie in the bullpen, I was also glad. I want to see whether the warm-up pitcher has his deliveries under control. Maglie, a pitcher with pinpoint accuracy, likes to work his two different speed curve balls down low and his fast ball inside on the hands or at the shoulders. As I watched him, he was either experimenting with other stuff or else was woefully off. He was throwing his curves too high and his fast ball either far inside or far outside.

There is an old standby in baseball that has directed pitchers for decades: Keep the curve low and the fast ball high. That way, the curve ball is hit into the dirt and the fast ball popped up. There is nothing hard and fast about this rule, but it is more true than false. Maglie, however, was unable to follow the advice. Once he stopped, shook his head for a moment, took a deep breath and tugged at his belt. I imagined that he was worried.

His mound opponent, Bob Lemon, was working in the usual spot reserved for the visiting team starting pitcher, in foul territory slightly behind and to the third-base side of home. Lemon seemed to have his stuff, especially a low-breaking pitch that was coming in and down from right to left as I viewed it, or from left to right as the catcher squatted. I was afraid the right-handed hitters on the Giants were going to have their hands full with this pitch. However, Lemon, like Maglie, seemed to have no speed to speak of, and I assured myself that in time his down-curve would straighten itself out.

A popular band had been playing out in center field all during practice, featuring Latin rhythms in general and a hippy shimmying female vocalist in particular. She would rotate on the bandstand and then stand too close to the microphone and yell. The amplifier is at the top of the dressing room above the bleachers, and much too near for comfort. I longed for the old Regimental Armory band that used to play at such functions, but apparently today the show is the thing.

The band once played, "Say Hey," the song inspired by the expression alleged to be used by Mays. It was the first time I had ever heard the song, though for the last five months or so I have been singing a little ditty of my own invention to my daughter; I called it "Say Hey, Willie." Some of my lyrics, which change from day to day, are, "Say Hey, Willie; Say Hey, Willie Mays; Say Hey, Willie; How do you make them plays? Say Hey, Willie; Runnin' outta your hat; Say Hey, Willie; Whatcha mean by that?" My song seemed no worse than the official one.

Finally the players came out of their dugouts and stood at attention along the foul lines while Perry Como perched on the bandstand to croon, "The Star-Spangled Banner." He sang it quite pleasantly except for stretching the word "land" in the next to last line for three syllables instead of the usual two. Como received polite applause for his stint and as he walked across the field to a third-base box seat, I was pleased that there were no conspicuous squeals of female delight. It meant that the little girl brigade was absent and the game would not be mortified by those shrill cheers that salute every pop fly.

Now came an announcement about some boy throwing out the first pitch, but I didn't hear it quite right and somehow never did get to see him throw the ball.

Then the Giants swarmed out of their dugout, led by Alvin Dark, their captain and shortstop, and Maglie sauntered to the pitching mound, that slight hill that rises in a round brown patch out of the slick grass of the infield. And the game began.

49

FOUR

Maglie immediately bore out my doubts as to his control. He was badly off with his first two pitches, missed the outside corner by a slight margin with his third, and then plunked the Cleveland leadoff hitter, Al Smith, in the ribs with the fourth. There is a saying in baseball, "A walk is as good as a hit." I think that a walk to the first hitter of any inning is better (for the offensive team) than a hit. A hit is a hit is a hit, but a base on balls makes you wonder whether your pitcher will get his control back, makes you wonder whether he'll get tight and groove a fat pitch to the next man, makes you wonder whether the other team will wait out the pitcher and force him to throw and throw until his arm starts to ache. A base on balls is a goddamn nuisance at least to this spectator. Hitting Smith on the three-and-no count was about the same as a base on balls.

Then, with the same resilient optimism that I had been carrying around all day, I recalled that in the other World Series game I saw, the only other one I ever saw, the first batter walked and that team lost. So I had another omen.

I yelled, not seriously, "That's all right, Sal. If you're going to walk him, you might as well hit him at the same time."

The woman in the red hat whirled around and said, "There you go again, there you go." Then she turned to the diamond and screamed, "Tear 'em apart, Indians." She sat down.

When Maglie's next pitch to Avila, the American League batting champion, was high, you could see a stirring in the Giant dugout and when Avila poked a not too severe line drive into right field that was fumbled by Mueller, allowing Smith to go to third, the stirring increased until Don Liddle got up and took off his jacket in the bullpen and began warming up.

The next batter was Doby. The woman in the red hat, a Dodger fan rooting against the hated Giants (though I rooted for the Dodgers against the Yankees in 1953), yelled, "Hit it where you live, Larry."

I knew that Doby hailed from Paterson, New Jersey, and my calculations were that Paterson was in foul territory, almost directly behind the plate. I did not bother to mention this to her because I have long ago ceased trying to reason with Dodger fans.

A man directly behind me, however, said, "Hit the light tower in right field, Larry," and I felt I had to retort to this.

I said, "Hit the light tower at second base, Larry." I do not pretend that there is any sparkling wit in any of this byplay, but it is all part of the struggle wherein we fans carry invisible bats and take invisible hitches at our belts, spit on our hands and chew huge wads of tobacco. Though we are patently the watchers, we are really the participants, as the racing heart attests, the tight chest, the rushing blood hot in the temples.

Thus it was not just a battle between Maglie and Doby, or the Giants and the Indians. At that moment of light-tower remarks, we were engaged in a three-way silent war, a woman in a red hat, a man behind me whom I had never seen, and I. Doby resolved the battle in indefinite fashion by popping the ball to Henry Thompson, the Giant third baseman, who caught the ball in foul territory. The Paterson woman had the right direction and I had about the right distance. The man behind me was a poor last.

However, the result was what I wanted, so feeling it would be a good day I yelled to the next batter, Al Rosen, "Hit it to the first base light tower, Al." He promptly popped the ball to Whitey Lockman, a few feet from first base.

By this time, I felt nothing would go wrong. I was like a man who had shot two sevens in dice and lets it go to his head. I recall now a football game when I was a student at De Witt Clinton in which I made the chance remark, all-hope and no-basis, that a Clinton halfback (I named him) was going to run around his right end and go eighty yards for a touchdown. He did, on the very next play. A man next to me who was betting quarters with another man gave me a queer look and said, "Stick around, kid. You may be useful."

I do not know how useful I was because I made rash predictions on practically every play thereafter and none of them was correct.

I should have recalled that incident at the series, and kept my mouth shut. Instead, I bet all my money (as invisible as the bat I carry or the tobacco I chew) on the next man, Vic Wertz. Wertz is a large left-handed hitter who used to be a terrifying batter when he was with the Detroit Tigers but who had been traded to other teams when his batting average dipped. I shouted, "All right, Vic. Hit it

52

Larry Doby, center fielder

to the catcher." This meant I wanted him to strike out.

Instead Wertz hit a triple well over Mueller's head in deep right field, and the Indians were two runs ahead.

The woman in the red hat was briefly unbearable and the man behind me—the Cleveland fan—did the completely unethical. In all the din he managed to clap me on the back. I snarled, twisting my head but still disdaining to look at him, "Can it, Mac! We'll get 'em back."

I fully expected that "we" would, but two runs down before the first half of the first inning is complete does not contribute to a heart swelling with gladness or a love for your fellow being.

I said, a bit impatiently, I'm afraid, "All right, Sal, wrap it up. Let's get out of here."

Maglie wrapped it up as neatly as he could, after all that damage, by forcing Dave Philley, the Indian right fielder, to hit a long drive to Don Mueller, on which the Giant this time did not err. It was, however, a well-hit ball and my alarm was by now quite large.

Still, I was confident that two runs would not beat the Giants. The problem would be not so much in getting the runs back, as in holding in further check what appeared to be an explosive Indian attack. Dull-witted they may be, I thought, slow and timid, but they swing the bat. Goddamn American Leaguers.

Though sour grapes back up such foolish anger, there also is some truth in it. The American League—during and since Ruth—had spoiled the old-time kind of game. With one swish of the bat, well-pitched, tightly defended games were smashed out of sight, and the American Leaguers— those brash muscular youngsters—had developed most of the big swishers. Ruth, Gehrig, Foxx, Greenberg, Williams —there is no similar quintet to be found in the annals of the National League. Ott, yes, and Mize, and Hornsby

54

(not a great slugger, actually, but a great hitter), Kiner and, to an even lesser degree, Musial—they are the big stickmen of the older, gentler, superior-in-every-other-way circuit. And, of course, Chuck Klein, who hit so many home runs in that tiny old Philadelphia ball park where thick-handled bats predominated because any pop fly off the handle of a bat stood a decent chance of falling over the right-field wall.

So Maglie's problem, and the Giants' (and perforce, mine) was to hold off the big hitters while the Giants whittled away at the two-run disparity.

In my omen-clutching mood and to balance my despair, I recalled how Maglie had yielded two runs to the Dodgers in the first inning of a vital game earlier this season, and then shut out Brooklyn the rest of the way. Come to think of it, in each game of that three-game series (one of the many series during the pennant campaign which the sports-writers deemed "crucial," a term so overworked that they sometimes must spell it "crooshal" or something equally painful)—in each game the Dodgers had scored twice in the first inning only to see the Giants win in a walk. The solution might be, then, for the Giants always to allow the opposition two runs in the first inning.

And in their half of the first inning, it appeared that the Giants would get the runs back right then and there. In a game that was to be full of surprises, Whitey Lockman surprised me on the very first pitch. And so did the In-dians.

Lockman bunted the ball past the pitcher's mound and toward second base, the kind of bunt that is usually im-possible to field before the runner crosses first base. It was a perfect bunt, and Lockman is a speedy man. So I yelled, "Attaboy, Whitey," once the immediate surprise had passed, and then I watched in stunned silence as Bobby

Avila swooped down, picked up the ball on the dead run, and threw Lockman out at first.

Well, I thought, they swing the bat *and* they field. A dim notion was entering my scarred old brain as to why the Indians had been able to win one hundred and eleven games, a notion that had little to do with the weakness of the American-League second division.

But I gave myself little time for pessimism. Al Dark squatted in the batter's box and began to squirm in that nervous ungraceful manner that so marks his hitting. Dark has a further habit that disconcerts me. He occasionally swings at pitches over his head. But I am a Dark fan and have come to accept the many flaws in his mechanical makeup. They are the flaws one found in Pepper Martin and more recently in Eddie Stanky, and Dark is superior to either, withal.

In appreciation of my silent vote of confidence, Dark refrained from swinging at pitches that were not in the strike zone, and in time Lemon served four balls.

That tiny stirring inside me was reflex. I have no more control over it than a lion has over his saliva when he sees a crippled zebra lying before him. I muttered to no one in particular, "Let's tie it up, Don."

American League-itis again, of course, this foolish reliance on brute power. To tie it up right now, Mueller would have to hit a home run. Now, Mueller is possibly the most improved ball player in the league, with the exception of his own teammate, Mays. In years past, Mueller did some lusty hitting, but not too much, and in the field he committed such atrocious blunders that before each new season, Manager Durocher announced a different rookie as his starting right fielder. One year it was even to be Clint Hartung, a pitcher who couldn't pitch too well, and an outfielder who couldn't catch flies too well.

56

But each season, Mueller's talent for slicing singles and doubles to left and left-center field won back his place in the lineup. Giant fans then fell into two camps, those who thought Mueller's hitting ability outweighed his inability to go back for fly balls, and those who did not. I belonged to both camps; for the first half of a season, I was a "did-not." Over the final half, I was a "did." Of course, Mueller's early-season jitters and poor judgment on long flies must have stemmed from Durocher's stubborn refusal to allow the poor man time to get used to right field. It must be difficult to learn to catch fly balls while sitting on a bench between home plate and first base. If fielding practice were still a serious business, Mueller might have so adapted himself that he could glide smoothly out to right field at the first Durocher whim and comport himself without too much awkwardness.

This season Durocher had no rookie to inflict on Mueller. So Mueller promptly became an acceptable fielder, and though his throwing arm is not in Mays' class, he made as many assists in 1954 as did Mays. Naturally, runners hesitate to advance on Mays' arm, whereas they have fewer qualms concerning Mueller's.

At the plate there seldom had been any criticism of Mueller. He is so versatile a hitter that exuberant baseball announcers began to call him "Mandrake," after the magician. His style is somewhat similar to that of Bill Terry, my very favorite of all ball players, a man who had great power but who also learned to spray his hits to any field. Mueller is not as good as Terry, nor does he have the raw power, but he does go on occasional binges of slugging, once hitting five home runs against the Dodgers over a two-day period. Sentimentalists may take heart in the fact that Mueller became a father just before the first of those five home runs.

Still, it was wishful thinking and that symptom of the American League which led me to mutter, "Let's tie it up," as Mueller lightly held his bat off his shoulder. Only a home run could tie the score and Mueller had not again become a father on this World Series day. I saw Mueller hit his first home run of 1954 and it occurred well along in the campaign. He hit it against Pittsburgh, and there is very little in Lemon that reminds you of Pittsburgh pitchers.

I didn't even have faith in my own words, and disowned them on the spot. I nudged the man on my right, not the casino player who by this time had revealed himself as equally inept in watching a ball game as in playing cards, and I said, "Watch this. He's going to hit to left field." I meant a slicing hit, a single or possibly a double, but not a home run.

I had studied Mueller and triumphantly knew his intention. Mueller's attitude at the plate was one of thoughtfulness, not power, as he held the bat as though he were weighing it. He usually keeps his hands a few inches above the end of the bat and he delivers his swing with a snap of his wrists rather than a long sweep of his arms.

So Mueller whacked the ball to right field, taking a full sweeping swing with his arms, and Dark raced around to third base.

Now I had reason to yell words about tying it up. The tying run was on first base, the leading run at the plate. The man representing the leading run was Willie Mays.

I said, "Hey, Willie, let's show 'em."

I saw the woman in the red hat glance apprehensively over at the left-field bullpen. She had a slightly better view of it than I. I asked her, "Anybody warming up?"

58

and she shook her head in the negative. It was as though we did not hate each other.

Mays lashed his bat back and forth in Lemon's direction, and Lemon, with a placid dignity utterly lacking in Maglie, stood off to the side of the mound, staring at the baseball in his hand. Dignity, of course, has never struck out a man.

Mays is, as everybody knows, and as Lemon undoubtedly knew more keenly than anyone, the National League batting champion. He is the champion of both leagues, in fact, though it is foolish to so designate him since he faced only National League pitching. Still, his league has most of the fine pitchers and it is my feeling that Mays would have hit .375 in the American League. But this is a matter of idle conjecture, because Lemon now made him pop the ball softly to George Strickland, the Indian shortstop.

After this, the elated feeling went leaking out of the stands like air from a balloon. Nobody expected Henry Thompson to make a hit, and he didn't.

And so "we" were two down at the end of the first inning, and though I said with loud confidence, "That's all right. Eight more shots at 'em," my pre-game buoyancy now felt heavy as lead.

In the second inning, Maglie made the switch that has been associated with his pitching for the past few years. His curve ball was behaving and he got two curves past Indian hitter, George Strickland. Then he fooled the shortstop with a rare fast ball and struck him out. Catcher Jim Hegan, a tall, graceful fellow, followed with a little fly ball to Henry Thompson, and though Lemon (a more dangerous hitter than most pitchers because he used to play other positions) walked, young Smith was also struck out.

59

The Giant half was not notable for any great uprising, although Wes Westrum, the team's weakest hitter with the exception of Maglie, singled sharply.

The eight Giant shots had now been reduced to seven, and the game was entering that lull period which some people find boring but which I find lengthens the buildup before the final crackling climax or climaxes. The longer and more quiescent the lull, the more emphatic seem the climaxes; it is the tightening of the screw, the technique of suspense that is stamped so firmly on all Hitchcock films.

Of course, sometimes the lull extends too far, and the last out has been recorded before any crackling climax can occur. We have then watched what amounts to a dull game. But even within the structure of a dull game, there is so much to be seen—the pitching, the unfolding of defensive patterns, the mobility and unbelievable coordination of a double play—that most lovely of all defensive feats of athletic collaboration. Just the sight of a routine grounder to shortstop is exciting. The ball must be played perfectly—not just pretty well, but perfectly—otherwise a swift runner will have an infield hit. The moving to the ball, the scoop, the set position, the throw—and the first baseman's sweeping stretch into the diamond, all this must be executed with a minimum of activity and cover a minimum of time. And nine innings full of such stuff! Routine is surely the wrong word, and so is dull.

Not that I expected this game to be "dull" in any respect.

In the Indian third, against three of the team's more dangerous hitters, Avila, Doby, and Rosen, the ball was not once hit out of the infield. Maglie's skill restored my spirits. I waited for the ax to fall on Lemon.

And in that third inning, the Giants, who had pecked

away at Lemon in each of their previous bats, got the two runs back. By studying my program of the first two and a half innings, it becomes apparent that the Giants were on the verge of "reaching" Lemon, that sooner or later they would break through. With the exception of Irvin who had raised a foul pop to the catcher, every man had come around on the ball and hit it to his "power" field. That is, the right-handed hitters had pulled the ball to the left-field side of the diamond, and the left-handed hitters to the right-field side, like tennis players hitting cross-court smashes. This meant they were not swinging late, which verified my opinion of Lemon's lack of speed. It also meant that the sharp down-curve Lemon throws to right-handed hitters was still being pulled.

The ultimate importance of such "pulling" lies in the way the Polo Grounds is built. The fences at the right and left-field foul lines lie within easy striking distance, but as they fall away to center field, the possibility of driving a ball over those fences becomes quite remote. Home runs are made at the Polo Grounds by pulling the ball down the line, the way Doby was doing in hitting practice. The Giants were—even this early and with no runs to show for it—giving evidence of an ability to pull Lemon's pitches. Sooner or later, one of these pulled pitches would surely end up in the stands.

The Indians, on the other hand, were hitting mostly to the "opposite" or "wrong" field—right handers hitting to the right side the way golfers slice, and left handers to the left, with the noisy exception of Wertz and Philley.

I explained this simple theory to the casino player who looked at me rather blankly and said, "Two runs is two runs." I thought: to hell with you, Mac, I hope you play casino for money some time.

The evidence in support of my contention piled up in

61

the Giant third. Lockman singled sharply to right field, and Dark began writhing away in the batter's box. Lemon threw that wonderful down-curve to Dark, a breaking ball that seemed headed for the dirt on the first-base side of home plate. But because Whitey Lockman was running with the delivery of the pitch—the famous hit-and-run play that is the offensive equal in drama and skill to the double-play—Dark had to swing at the ball, or else risk Lockman's being thrown out stealing by Hegan. It was a pitch that could not be hit to left field, and, indeed, Dark would not have wanted to do so—that would have placed the ball in front of Lockman where an outfielder would have had a shorter throw to make to third base.

Dark did not hit it to left field. He lashed it past the startled Lemon who was not used to seeing such pitches hit at all, and the ball sped merrily over second base. Lockman easily reached third.

I bellowed with the crowd, and I do not remember what I said or what they were saying, if they were saying sense at all. Not a run had been scored by the Giants, yet the noise was three, possibly four times as loud as the noise that accompanied Wertz's triple in the first inning. The crowd was warming up.

So too was an Indian pitcher.

I stood and leaned far forward and I could now see the number "1" on the back of a Cleveland uniform as a ball was being lobbed to a bullpen catcher out of sight. I turned hastily to my program. The "1" meant the pitcher was Art Houtteman, number 11, because the only other pitcher whose double-number ends in "1" is Lemon, number 21, standing on the mound as he prepared to pitch to Mueller. Number 1 itself belongs to Avila, and 31 to Wally Westlake, an injured, benched outfielder. It had to be Houtteman.

I yelled something to the effect that the Lemon was plenty sour, and somebody else picked up the theme and said, "They're sure putting the squeeze on Lemon." The woman in the red hat turned around and said something that sounded like, "Aw, go shovel it," and the Cleveland fan directly behind—who had committed the cardinal sin of slapping my back as though I were on his side—was saying quietly, over and over, "Everything's all right, Bobby boy, everything's all right, Bobby boy." He sounded ill.

Then Lemon was leaning forward to study catcher Hegan's sign, and the rest of us leaned with him, most of us hoping the Indian hurler would not be able to pitch his way out of his difficulty, a handful of fans hoping he would.

He almost did, but not quite. Mueller hit a bounding ball sharply to Avila at second who threw it to Strickland who in turn threw it to Wertz at first. But Mueller beat this latter throw, and though the inning's first out had been made, a run scored.

Once more it was up to Mays to continue the offensive. Lemon, who is a courageous man, is also a wisely cautious man, and in his caution this time he lost Mays, walking him on four pitches. Mueller moved to second.

And now, whereas nobody had expected Henry Thompson to get a hit in the first inning when a runner was in scoring position with two out, this time hopes were high. The reason is obvious, I think. Mays in the first inning had made out. We all felt let down. This time Mays had worked Lemon for a walk, keeping the inning alive and, in fact, contributing heavily to it. All Thompson had to do now was catch the fever that swept the stands.

He did. He drove a slashing ground ball past first baseman Wertz into right field (once again the ball had been pulled), and the second Giant run scampered home. Mays

63

ran around second on the hit and slid into third ahead of Philley's throw, losing his cap in the process. Outside of Mays' basket catch, nothing else so identifies the young Giant as the sight of his cap flying off.

The inning which seemed still to hold so much promise quickly died, however, when Irvin struck out and Davey Williams was out on a grounder.

But the game was back on an even footing.

In the Indian fourth, Wertz made another hit. Then after Philley had tapped feebly to Maglie and was thrown out, enabling Wertz to move down to second, Maglie started to work on Strickland.

One of his pitches was outside and suddenly Westrum was standing up and snapping a throw past the box, down to second base where Davey Williams was trying to get behind Wertz. It was a pick-off play, but it failed on many counts. Wertz, for one thing, was within a step or two of the base when Westrum began his throw. Then too the throw was on the third-base side of the bag, and in the suddenly crowded conditions—big Wertz, little Williams, and the ball all at more or less the same place at the same time—the ball bounced off the heel of Williams' glove and rolled away.

Fortunately it rolled not too far and Wertz was satisfied with brushing the new accumulation of dirt from his trouser leg.

Otherwise the first half of the fourth was a model inning for the Giants. Maglie's short wrenching motion with his right arm had the ball acting nicely now, and his control had become a thing of beauty. The right-handed Indian hitters found themselves falling away from inside pitches that suddenly veered across the corner of the plate. Too late they would chop at the ball and hit it meekly into the air or harmlessly on the ground. Of the first twelve

64

Indians retired, only one hit to the outfield, and that in the first inning.

And in the Giant half of the fourth inning, Lemon was threatened with rout once more.

Westrum, who had hit a savage ground ball past the bare-hand side of Al Rosen in the second inning, now opened the fourth with an equally hard-hit ball to the gloved-hand side of the Indian third baseman. On each instance, Rosen left his feet, sprawling on his belly and face as he tried to stop the ball. I am always delighted to see anybody give out with the old college try, and in this case I was doubly delighted because it failed signally to stop the flight of either ball.

Here Maglie tried to bunt the ball so that Westrum could advance to second, but three attempts resulted in nothing more worthy than a foul ball, and a strikeout.

The importance of Lemon's victory over Maglie in this tiny duel was made manifest when Lockman grounded out to Wertz while Westrum advanced to second. Al Dark continued to plague Rosen, this time with another sharply rapped ground ball to his left. Rosen made a fine lunging grab of the ball and then whirled and threw hurriedly and inaccurately to Wertz. The first baseman had to come away from the bag to catch the throw, and Dark was safe. The blow was scored as a base hit because Dark would have beaten Rosen's throw, even had it been true.

By this time Westrum had reached third base. Had Maglie's bunt been successful, the catcher would have arrived there one out earlier and scored on Dark's hit.

But "if" is a mighty big word; in this case it was ninety feet long. For Mueller made the third out, and the Giants didn't score despite my further derogatory remarks to Lemon that he was being squashed to a pulp.

FIVE

As the game approached the halfway mark, I looked around at the stadium for the first time since before game time. It was, as I knew, filled. Earlier there had been a few available seats behind pillars, but the standees must have taken them now. It was a capacity crowd, but World Series contests usually have so many free admissions— "dead heads" as they are so fondly termed—that the announced paid attendance is never quite what one expects. This seemed just about as large a crowd as the one on a Memorial Day back in the '30's when I and 60,000 other people saw the Giants beat the Dodgers twice at the Polo Grounds. Today I am baffled as to why 60,000 people were interested in seeing the Dodgers in those days unless it was to watch the Dodger fastball pitcher, Van Lingle Mungo. If that was the reason, then we were all disappointed. Van Mungo was knocked out of the box in a five-run first inning of the first game. I don't think he got a man out.

Since that date, however, fire regulations have become

more rigidly enforced, and fewer standees are now permitted. But by any standard, this was a great crowd that I viewed.

It had become, however, a quiet crowd, an attitude that was remarked on in puzzlement by some reporters in the next day's papers. Actually, most tight pitchers' duels are quiet affairs, and the noise that occurs when a pitcher, especially the home-team pitcher, gets the last out in an inning while enemy runners languish on the base paths is not a loud noise but rather a whooshing sound of relief.

Such were the noises that attended the final Cleveland outs in the fifth and sixth innings.

In the fifth, pitcher Lemon led off by lofting a high drive to left-center field, not too deep to cause trouble, especially when the outfielder is Mays. Still it meant that Mays had to run to his right and back a short distance, and he caught the ball up at the level of his cap instead— as is his wont—at his beltline, his glove palm up. It was Mays' first chance and a rather routine one (that silly word "routine" again; have *you* ever tried to run forty feet to catch a baseball that has traveled some three hundred and thirty feet in length and has described an arc about a hundred feet high?)—and the fans made none of the hullabaloo that they would have made were they Yankee fans and the outfielder DiMaggio, or Milwaukee fans and the outfielder anybody in a Brave uniform.

Probably the fans here were a bit disappointed with the Mays catch. During the regular season, Mays must have made thirty catches each of which caused somebody—usually the disgruntled batter—to say it was the best catch ever made.

After Lemon went out, Al Smith was badly fooled by a Maglie curve at his hands—and as a result, got himself a base hit. Smith swung over the pitch, barely grazing it and sending the ball on a slow roll down the third base line. Both Henry Thompson and Maglie moved in on the ball, but when Thompson picked it up, Smith was crossing first base.

Then Avila lifted another "routine" fly to left field which Monte Irvin played badly but caught, clutching the ball in a lunging, awkward gesture.

The man behind me shouted, "Hey, Monte, when you going to start wearing glasses?"

The remark made me feel bad, and I growled over my shoulder, "He don't need glasses. A team of blind men could beat them bums."

I don't know why I fall into speech such as that, but I do. Probably it is some compensation, some complex about not being one of the gang, some form of inverted snobbism.* I dislike myself for talking that way.

For another thing, I was a complete hypocrite when I growled up my ungrammatical rejoinder; the man behind me was expressing my exact thought. I, too, was wondering whether Irvin's eyesight had gone back on him a trifle.

But I had no time to worry about Irvin. A moment later I had all the Giants to fret over. Doby was up, frightening me with his swing. When he hit a Maglie pitch, I prepared to wince, but Doby broke his bat on the pitch, and though the ball looped into the outfield, all he had for that tremendous swing was a single. Right now—I said to myself—I'll settle for a single every time he comes up. I feel the same way about Stan Musial, with even better reason. Every time I see him play, he hits a home run.

On Doby's broken-bat single, Smith displayed considerable speed—in contrast to his mates—and easily

---

* My wife says it is because I am a slob.

Bobby Avila, second baseman

made it into third base. Once more Don Liddle got up to throw some practice tosses in the Giant bullpen, and as Maglie fiddled out there on the mound, a right hander joined Liddle. This had to be either Hoyt Wilhelm or Marv Grissom. It was Grissom.

Maglie, however, was not through. He induced Al Rosen to hit a third fly, to the third outfielder, Mueller, and the inning was over, the whooshing sound sweeping through the stands.

In the sixth inning, big Wertz, who had hit the first-inning triple and a fourth-inning single to left field, now turned his attention back to right with a line drive base hit that landed in front of Don Mueller. Mueller then made a smart play, but he made it poorly. Wertz thundered into first base and made the usual wide turn that enables a runner to keep some momentum going without getting too far from first. The maneuver invariably results in the outfielder's throwing the ball with haste to the next station, forcing the runner back to the base he has already reached.

On this occasion, however, Mueller threw behind the runner. Had the throw been true, Wertz might have been caught off the base, had first baseman Lockman been on the bag. But baseball doesn't usually allow you one "if," much less two. The throw from Mueller went over the head of Lockman (who wasn't on the bag anyway) and rolled toward the plate.

In baseball, errors have a way of compounding themselves. Having taken his chance and muddled it, Mueller now had to pay, and with him, the Giants. For Westrum, usually so alert at the plate, was in the process of either picking up his glove or his mask as the ball dribbled toward him.

70

In the bleachers, over five hundred feet from Westrum, I felt that same miserable frustration of a man who watches a holdup but is too far away to warn the victim. Once when I was a tot, I saw a Charlie Chaplin film—*Shoulder Arms*, I think—wherein Charlie was menaced by some foreign figure stealing up behind him. Enthralled and frightened, I yelled from my balcony seat, "Look out, Charlie!" Needless to say, Charlie didn't hear me.

So, mutely this time, I watched Westrum and the ball skipping gaily toward him. Suddenly the Giant catcher spotted it, made a lunge and missed. The ball continued its dribble onward, and Wertz, who had hesitated at first, now set out for second. Westrum captured the ball before it rolled into the Cleveland dugout and thereby prevented Wertz from reaching third automatically. A faster man, even without the automatic grant, would have tried for third and probably made it, but Wertz is not a fast man.

I said, "Can't understand that Westrum."

The casino player looked up and said, "That's not Westrum, that's Wertz." As I said before, he was not a perceptive person.

"No," I said, nettled at him, at Mueller, at Westrum, and, of course, at Wertz, "I mean letting the ball roll past him." It was a sloppy play and I wondered whether the Giants were going to lapse into a botched-up inning.

"That's Mueller's fault," the casino player said.

I should have remained silent, but my wife has introduced me to the better-get-it-off-your-chest school, so I thought I would be happier if I expressed my irritation to and at the casino player, even though he was a Giant fan. I cannot abide stupid Giant fans. Thank goodness there are so few.

"I know it was Mueller's fault. Still Westrum should have got to the ball sooner."

He said, the voice of perfect logic, "But there was no play at the plate."

The man behind me said, "That's what Mueller gets, being a hog. Must think he's Furillo."

The woman in the red hat said, "He should live so long."

I said, "Furillo should have the money Mueller's making today." I meant Mueller's World Series share, which had been estimated before the game at either eight or ten thousand dollars, depending on whether the Giants won or lost.

The woman in the red hat chose deliberately to misunderstand. "Furillo gets a bigger salary than Mueller," she said.

I decided I had been beaten by everybody in sight and a few out of sight. I shut up.

The reason we had so much time for this colloquy was that Wertz, at second base, was engaged in what seemed to be a time-wasting gesture aimed at rattling Maglie, a feat that not even Jackie Robinson has been able to pull off with any large success. Wertz was bent over, playing with his pants and/or upper sock, I could not tell which.

A Giant fan yelled, "What's the matter, Woitz, out of breat'? Gettin' old, Woitz?"

I'd have hated to see Wertz any younger or spryer than he had been in this game so far.

Actually, as it was revealed in the next day's papers, Wertz wears a fiber shin guard on his left leg, protection against being hit by his own foul drives while batting. When Wertz ducked back into first on Mueller's throw,

72

the clasp on the guard flew open. Then as he ran to second, the guard—which weighs about a pound—flapped against his leg. And because he did not want to risk tripping on the flapping guard, he remained at second.

This is the kind of luck that has been part of the Giants' showing all through 1954.

Still, the inning was not over, and the Indians had a man in scoring position. A normal hit will score most runners from second, even those whose shin guards flap loose.

But after Wertz comes to bat, the lower, weaker part of the Indian batting order must make its appearance. I do not recall that anyone in the next day's papers or over the radio that evening (after an important Giant victory, I read all the papers and listen to all the sports commentators with great gloating)—I do not recall anyone noting that the sixth, seventh, eighth, and ninth places in the Indian lineup failed to make a hit all that first day, contributing instead a total of sixteen putouts. Only four of these outs reached the outfield.

It is astonishing that so poorly balanced an attack as this could have helped win one hundred and eleven games during the season. Such imbalance pays tribute to the fine pitching of the Indians; it also pounds home with disparaging gestures the feebleness of the rest of the American League.

The sixth man, Dave Philley, drove a hard ground ball back at Maglie that appeared to hit either the rubber slab or Maglie's foot. The pitcher quickly fell on the ball and threw it to first to retire Philley. Wertz moved to third. The seventh man, George Strickland, a National-League castoff, hit a pop fly to Alvin Dark. This was the "important" out because now it would take a hit or some defensive miscue to score Wertz. Had Strickland managed to hit a decently long fly ball or a high-bounding, slowly hit ground ball, Wertz would have lumbered in with the tie-breaking run.

Now it was up to Hegan, eighth man in the Indian lineup. Hegan also made out, but he did so in more exciting fashion. He hit a sharp bounding ball to the right of Henry Thompson, along the third-base line. Thompson is a third baseman of two schools. One, he is a sure-glove man, not quite as sure as Billy Cox, perhaps, but not far behind, and probably far ahead of everybody else. And two, he fights the ball very much like Pepper Martin, wrestling it to the ground, pinning it to make sure it doesn't get away, and then flinging it to first, just in time. Thompson has a fine, strong arm but once in a while he demonstrates this too clearly by throwing the ball to the first-base box seats.

This time, on Hegan's bounder, Thompson employed the tactics of both schools, minus the conclusive proof of his strength. He darted to his right, brought his glove to his right hip and smothered the drive that could easily have gone on past and into the left-field corner where it would have been an easy two-base hit.

But even a one-base hit, an infield single, would be drastic at this stage, and Thompson, once having slowed down the ball, now switched to school two. He dove after the ball, stopped its squirming rolling progress in foul territory, got back to his feet, and threw it as hard as he could—but accurately—to the outstretched glove of Lockman. Hegan was out by a full stride, and the inning was over.

The speed with which a man like Thompson operates is amazing when one considers that it takes a fast man about four seconds to run from home plate to first after he has hit the ball, a slow man about five seconds. In these

74

four to five seconds, Thompson had taken a few short steps, then gone to the ground, got up and thrown the baseball one hundred and twenty-five feet.

The inning was over and once more, the whooshing sound sighed through the stadium, a trifle higher pitched, a trifle noisier. It was obvious that the game was nearing a point of tension where something probably would snap. Nobody—I'm sure—expected it to snap and build and snap and build so often, as it did in the last few innings.

SIX

So much for the Indians in the fifth and sixth. Still, I had been shaken. The Indians seemed to be the team doing the reaching of the opposing pitcher. Lemon, on the other hand, suddenly stopped being hit. He had yielded seven hits in the first four innings and at no time during that period did it appear that he would manage to last the route. In the fifth, however, Mays, Thompson, and Irvin were easy for the right hander who now was practically never throwing the ball higher than the waist. For the second time, Mays failed to hit the ball past the shortstop. Thompson struck out. Irvin, who had earlier struck out, now hit a rare Lemon fast ball meekly to center field where Doby caught it, and somebody muttered, "I don't know why they stick with that stiff."

There is no response to such a grumble. Durocher was not "sticking" with Irvin. He was playing him as his regular left fielder until such time as a bigger, hotter bat would be needed. If it were not needed, then Irvin served Durocher and the Giants better because—even with the one awkward grab earlier that inning—he played a better game defensively. Rhodes makes me nervous in left field, even more than the way Mueller used to make me nervous in right field. Those were my thoughts as Irvin trotted out to left field, but you do not voice such thoughts just as your champion has made out.

In the Giant sixth, Williams grounded out on a sharply hit ball to Strickland. Williams is the only Giant ignored by luck this past season. Game after game, I have seen him hit the ball sharply, but right at an infielder or on the line straight to an outfielder. It has become so sure that he will make out whenever my wife and I go to a game that she invariably says to me as Williams steps in, "Now, you don't really expect little Davey to get a hit, do you?"

I explain to her patiently that little Davey is ideally built for a light-heavyweight boxer, around five-ten and one hundred sixty-five or seventy pounds. I tell her that it is not because he is so tiny that his batting average is so low. I explain that he was no bigger in 1953 when he hit around .295. She listens and says, "You don't really expect him to hit, though, do you?"

It is because of such conversations that I said to my wife a few days before the series opened, "Don't be surprised if little Davey Williams is the hitting star of the whole shebang." She snorted.*

After Williams grounded out in the Giant sixth, Westrum came up. I *think* Westrum is the worst hitter playing regularly in major-league baseball. Certainly he is one of the five worst. Yet he is one of my favorites. He is a wonderful receiver, about as good as Campanella when Campanella is healthy, which is equivalent to the best around. Not the best ever. The best major-league catcher I've ever

* Williams went hitless throughout the entire series.

seen—that anyone's ever seen in the last quarter century —was Mickey Cochrane.

Major leaguer, that is. The all-round best was my Uncle Shorty when he played semi-pro ball with Cedarhurst, out on Long Island. He was the best catcher that ever played ball, I think, cat-quick, strong, graceful, with an incredibly accurate and powerful throwing arm.

Sadly, he could not hit curve-ball pitching, and more sadly, he was built all wrong. His legs were pipestem thin on a barrel of a body, and he had the nasty habit of breaking one of his legs on those rare occasions that he would slide into third base. This got to be so commonplace that one day when he closed his eyes and hit a curve ball over the right fielder's head and went sliding into third (too late), he never bothered to look down. It wasn't until he got up from the supper table that night, four or five hours later, that he realized he had broken his leg again.

Westrum is in that class of defensive catching. But at the plate, he cannot hit curve-ball *or* fast-ball pitching. And yet on this day, he had already rapped two singles, both well hit. This time I expected class to tell. Lemon would surely strike Westrum out, or overwhelm him in some manner. Instead the Giant catcher hit the ball even harder this time, a line drive that came winging out to center field, just a few feet to the right of Larry Doby. Doby caught it easily enough (though he appeared a trifle surprised), and the crowd ooh-ed and ah-ed.

When Westrum trotted back to the Giant dugout to don his catcher's gear, the fans sitting near the dugout between home and first clapped their hands in approval of his sudden burst of batting prowess.

The man behind me said, a whit sullenly, I think, "They cheer him for making out. What a ball club!"

78

Wes Westrum, catcher

I said mildly, "He hit the ball pretty damn good that time."

The man snorted.

I do not mind when my wife snorts at me. That is expected. But when some thick-skulled Cleveland fan snorts, then, by God, I am annoyed. I said, "Best-hit ball of the whole damn game." (It wasn't, but it wasn't far behind Wertz's blow of the first inning.)

He said, "Just a big out. Only a damn fool hits the ball to center field in this ball park."

That made sense, so I let it lie. I still hadn't seen the man's face.

I said to Maglie, who was stepping up to hit, "All right, Sal, get 'er started. This guy's getting soft."

The woman in the red hat said, "Somebody's getting soft in the head."

Maglie hit the ball about one-ninth as far and one-ninetieth as hard as had the other half of the Giant battery, rolling it between the pitcher's mound and first base. Wertz and Lemon handled the play nonchalantly, and Maglie stopped running halfway to first.

I said, "Attaboy, Sal, that's saving the old wind."

Had Maglie chosen to run like all get-out down the first-base line, I would undoubtedly have yelled, "Attaboy, Sal, that's the old spirit."

Actually, I was yelling less loudly because my throat was now starting to smart. It was going to be necessary for *me* to start saving the old wind.

Nearly two hours had gone by since the first pitch and the two teams were deadlocked. The sun, burning its way out of the yellow haze, now hung over the grandstand, edging along toward first base, and the shadows were creeping from the right-field foul area out to the diamond. The early-morning chill that I noted while standing on

80

line had been a brief affair, probably some dampness blowing in from the Harlem River. Now the day was warm, nearly hot, and the breeze, though still strong enough to ruffle the flags, was not cooling off the bleachers at all.

I carefully bit off the end of my second cigar, a Muriel, even though it had a perforated tip, and lit it. The beer man had one can of Ballantine in the midst of his regular brand, so I asked him for it. All around me, people were getting up, stretching and talking more loudly. There was an increased stream of coming and going along the ramp which leads to the rest room, but I'll be damned if I'll give in to cramped kidneys in the seventh inning of an all-even World Series game.

By tradition, the last half of the seventh is the stretch period, but because this makes it seem as though you are rooting for the home team when it comes to bat, visiting-team partisans have started a convention of their own, standing in the top half of the seventh inning. So now some home-team fans, like sheep, also get up in the first half of the inning. At least one in five in the bleachers was standing, some Indian, some Giant fans, some just plain stiff from sitting too long. I wanted to stand and stretch, but I felt it would be disloyal. I contented myself with drawing up my knees and then letting my legs drop.

SEVEN

As the spectators sat down again, the woman in the red hat said, "All right, Doby, you're going to hit a home run this inning." My eye raced down the program lineup and I saw that Doby would bat fourth in the inning, if he batted at all. It seemed likely that he would. In only one inning—the third—had Maglie retired Cleveland without allowing a man to reach first. His efforts in the past two innings were increasingly labored as though he were pushing the ball rather than throwing it. Maglie's motion is never a fluent one, but now it was looking tired, desperate, the throwing of a man who is made up of two parts, his right arm and his heart, and one of them was going fast.

In each of the past two innings, the Giant bullpen had been alerted, and Liddle and Grissom were sitting on the bench, hunched forward, watching intently the action on the field.

Doby, of course, was the man I feared, sore shoulder and all. His overpowering display of batting in the early practice was the hitting of a more than reasonably healthy

82

man, and it still lay graven on my mind. I, too, sat hunched forward, watching intently. The game had now reached that point where each action, each man coming up to bat, each pitch seemed so deliberate that you could almost imagine the individual player walking on a mountain of eggs, afraid to crack the first shell for fear of shattering all the others.

It was becoming a terribly long game, played at a dragging pace. Nearly any game Maglie pitches is a slow affair, for he takes so long between pitches. Once I timed him, knowing that the National League rules demand that there be no more than a twenty-second interval between pitches. During the inning I timed him, Maglie never got off a pitch inside the time limit. Once or twice it took him a full minute before he delivered.

After that I started timing several pitchers. Only Erv Palica and Reuben Gomez managed to abide by the rule, Palica sometimes taking as few as ten seconds between pitches. Somebody should tell Palica that he pitches too fast. He is one of the less successful pitchers in baseball.

Gomez, however, is one of the better, and he is a fast worker, especially when he is ahead of the batter, when there is nobody on base, and when his team is leading. But if his control falters or men get on, he takes the full twenty seconds and sometimes thirty.

Still Gomez is young and he has known only winning seasons. Not Maglie. So the fiddling goes on, the fidgeting and the time-consuming, and suppers are burned and wives' tempers are frayed, kiddies are bedded unkissed by fathers. It doesn't matter. When Maglie is on the mound, I don't care. Somehow his time-consuming manages to erase time as a factor; time stands still though the shadows creep toward the mound, and Maglie doesn't age. It is his little secret, and with him, I say to hell with the twenty-second rule. We'll take our Maglies slow and our suppers cold.

Not that Maglie is the only offender. The tempo of baseball itself has slowed down. As Maglie made more than the usual quota of practice pitches in that seventh inning, Lemon, the Indians' first hitter in the inning, stayed in the dugout until the umpire behind the plate turned and looked for him.

Then he came out, his bat held in his left hand, and the fans gave him a round of applause. Even I joined in that applause. It is meaningless in terms of attached loyalties. I hoped Lemon would strike out; it is perhaps fair to say that I would not have been particularly concerned if he had broken his leg in running out a ground ball. The next day I would have felt bad about it, sorry for Lemon and for the Indians and their misfortune, but at the moment my only desire was to see the Giants win.

Lemon neither struck out nor broke his leg. He hit a little fly ball behind shortstop that Dark grabbed and there was one out. After each out, I noticed that Maglie now turned his back on the plate, gaining his precious moment of relief, release possibly, before returning to the task at hand. It may be that even a Maglie must seek out the friendly tableau before he turns back to the snarling foe. More likely, Maglie was tired, and hoped that if he could conceal his fatigue and strain, the Indians would be less likely to seize upon his small distress and make capital of it. Since I did not take my wife's opera glasses, I do not know how Maglie looked when he turned toward the bleachers, but I can imagine the way he looked when he swung back again and faced the plate. I can imagine that he had wiped that drawn look from his face and replaced it with the ferocious scowl, the elastic lips pulled nearly straight down, the jaw outthrust and covered now with black sweat-shined stubble.

84

Bob Lemon, right-handed pitcher

One man was out in the seventh, and Doby would now bat only if Smith or Avila got on. Maglie threw his curve to Smith with that wrenching motion, and Smith hit it sharply to Henry Thompson's left. In the previous inning Thompson had made the one play incumbent on great third basemen: he had moved to his right, or bare-hand side, to make a stop and throw from the foul line, the longest throw a third baseman is usually called upon to make.

Now he had the less difficult, yet still touchy job of gliding to his left and keeping the bounding ball from going through into left field. He bent and swept the ball into his glove, and, while still moving to his left, threw Smith out at first. It was not a close play, but it was a fine one, punctuated at the receiving end by Lockman's forward and downward stretch to catch the low throw. The silence was broken by the crowd's roar, not exactly whooshy any more, more explosive. I threw my throat into the clamor.

Now Doby came out of the dugout and squatted in the little chalked circle near home plate. He would bat next, if Avila got on. I desperately hoped Avila wouldn't.

If I were a religious man, I might have prayed, but I don't think so. It seems to me that this brings into the fray an isolated morality factor that has no place in a baseball conflict. I understand that General George Patton once ordered an Army chaplain to write a prayer for a cessation of the rains that kept Allied planes grounded during Von Rundstedt's sudden dash through Ardennes during the Battle of the Bulge. The chaplain refused on the grounds that it was not in the realm of theology to pray for something to help kill your fellow man.

(Patton had the prayer written anyway, and signed his name to the back of it. The rain stopped.)

I felt like that chaplain on, of course, a far more limited

sphere. Who is there to say that the Giants deserve divine aid more than do the Indians? Of course I want them to win. But I do not feel in any way they *deserve* to win. It does not matter that they have been an unlucky team, in my eyes, for years and years. That will straighten itself out. And if it doesn't, it doesn't.

We Giant fans are stoical figures. When the pendulum pulls them to fifth place or lower, we sulk and hide, but I do not believe church attendance goes up. The Giants, so far as I know, are no more decent, no more law abiding, no more honest, no more kind to their wives and mothers and puppy dogs than any other team, including the Dodgers.

I remember once seeing a series of photographs showing Dodger first baseman Gil Hodges, at that time in a horrendous batting slump, shopping in a supermarket for his wife. Nothing could have made me feel a deeper kinship with Hodges who must surely be a patient, devoted man with a fine heart. (I am delighted to report that Hodges remained in his batting slump for nearly another year.)

Certainly Hodges and other non-Giants are worthy men. To pray, therefore, for divine intercession on behalf of the Giants would be presumptuous on my part, and an abuse of the powers of whatever God there may be.

Additionally, I think the rain in France would have stopped anyway. And I thought the Giants would win now no matter how often despair claimed me, or how often Doby batted or threatened to bat.

So I did not pray. But I *felt* like praying as Avila stepped in. I felt like muttering some incantation, weaving some spell that would put gaping holes in his bat. If Avila did not hit, then Doby would not bat until the eighth. There was inside of me a growing obsession that a home run would win the contest, and that Doby was going to hit a home run. I do not mean that the Giants would then lose. If I have to explain my way out of this, it is that I felt *a* home run would win the game, not the *only* home run, and that Doby would hit one. So would some Giant.

But I did not want the Indians to lead this late in the contest. And I especially did not want them to lead by two runs, as they would if Avila got on base and Doby hit that home run.

And so I said with a snap in my voice that I did not really feel, "All right, Sal, breeze it by this bum."

Then I leaned forward again, hunching my shoulders as though to draw a cloak around me and my fears. There was a brief chill when somebody quite a distance away— in the upper right-field deck, I believe—suddenly let loose a piercing howl, the only noise in the place for a second, and then Maglie was pushing the ball at Avila's hands and the second baseman (and American-League batting champion) was stepping forward and to the left with his front leg, the left one, and swinging smoothly, wickedly.

The Indian fans started to scream as they—and we—saw the blur of white whip down the third-base line, but before we heard the crack of the bat, Henry Thompson was falling to his knees, hands in front of him, and the line drive spattered into the pocket of his glove.

The first scream died, and the next one was born as Thompson got up and carelessly tossed the ball to the now-vacated mound as the Giants trotted from the field.

Doby hadn't batted. The Indian seventh was over and I felt a tired satisfaction as I stood and stretched.

EIGHT

A man was walking up the aisle during the stretch period, a man I thought I had seen before. He stopped at our row and looked past me to the man on the very end seat, sitting next to the wall between the bleachers and the left-field grandstand.

The man in the aisle said, "Well?"

The man at the end seat said, "Don't bother me. I just gave you some money last week."

The man in the aisle said, with a touch of exasperation, "That was for Mueller and it wasn't last week. This is for Hank Thompson. I just need two dollars more."

The other man said, "Sorry. Hit some other sucker."

The man trying to collect money said, "Cheapskate. Wait'll Hank hears about you."

The other man said, "Hank don't know me from Adam."

The man said, "Don't worry. He will." Then he looked at the rest of the row, barely passing me by and he shrugged his shoulders. "Bunch of cheapskates, all of ya."

The man to my right said, "He's still at it."

I said, "He's the guy who collects money to buy watches for Giant players?"

The fan on my right said, "Yeah. Imagine that. Giving money to him to buy a watch for Hank Thompson."

"Well," I said, "some fans chip in to buy a player a Cadillac."

"Ah," he said, "that's different."

I dropped it.

Suddenly the man was back, looking down our row. He said to no one in particular. "All right, who's kicking in? A nice watch for Shellenback. Come on, I need ninety bucks. Who's kicking in?"

Nobody looked at him. It was one of those painful moments that so often occur in the subway when a beggar jingles his cap in front of you and you try to look through him or make believe you're interested in the advertising cards. Everybody stared at the field and the self-appointed collector finally went off to another section of the bleachers. He had apparently got the two dollars for Thompson's watch. Now he was starting on Shellenback's. Shellenback is the Giant pitching coach. I wondered what made the man do a thing like that.

The fan next to me said, "A Cadillac is different."

"Aw," I said, "so is a yo-yo."

The man looked at me peculiarly, and I think he would have shifted a bit away from me if he had room.

I don't know why the whole thing irritated me, but it did. I don't blame the man for trying to collect the money. If he gets a kick out of it, why, then, it's his privilege. But the damn fools who pay to buy a watch for a ball player who is going to make at least eight thousand dollars in a week—that gets me. I reminded myself to ask my wife why they did it, and then why it got me so mad. I was sure she would know.°

° Concerning the people who chipped in, she said it was identification, vicarious pleasure, latent homosexuality, and unnatural.

90

By the time I had sat down, marking the end of intermission between halves of the seventh inning, I felt better. The Giants now had one batting turn more than the Indians, the seventh inning, as well as the eighth and ninth. So every time the Indians made out without scoring, the betting odds must have shifted to favor the Giants. Three licks to two is quite an advantage.

The last time I used this theory to boost my spirits was in 1951 when the Giants had clinched at least a tie for the pennant by beating Boston, and the Dodgers and Phillies were tied in their game down in Philadelphia. If the Dodgers lost, the Giants would have won the pennant. So each time the Dodgers made out in a late inning, I felt sure the Phils would win, especially when the game went into extra innings. Then Jackie Robinson hit a home run.

Still, I thought, remember the old law of averages. It stood to reason that the Giants were three-to-two favorites as they came up for the seventh. (If anybody had challenged me to bet, I would have wagered at even money. My money is seldom where my heart is.)

The inning opened quietly enough. Lockman grounded a high bouncer to Avila who threw easily to first. I had heard unkind things about Avila and his fielding, but thus far he had acquitted himself well in his defensive role. His play on Lockman's bunt in the first inning had been better than ordinary and at all other times he had been neat and quick in the field.

True, the only chance for a double play had been on a ground ball hit to Avila by the not-too-fast Mueller, and someplace along the way from second to shortstop

---

She said it made me mad because I wasn't the ball player getting the watch or the Cadillac. She said I could easily solve this by becoming a baseball player.

to first, the ball had slowed down enough to allow Mueller to reach first.

But there is no way of telling just where the potential double play missed connections. Maybe Avila did not scoop up the ball, turn and throw it to Strickland fast enough. Maybe Strickland did not charge across the base fast enough or get his throw off in time. Maybe Wertz, unused to playing first base after an entire career as an outfielder, did not stretch his body far enough into the diamond to reach the ball earlier.

Anyway on this play in the seventh inning, Avila looked graceful and sure, and as the Indians whirled the ball about the infield before returning it to Lemon, they all appeared graceful and sure, and terribly confident.

The Indians, like the Giants, are used to close contests. All season long they were falling behind in the opening and middle innings, and then closing the gap and finally winning in the late ones. There seemed to be no reason for their not being confident just now. Their pitcher looked as strong as he had been in the first inning, and his control was far sharper.

I said, "Let's get this guy. Come on, let's *get* him." But there was a note of near despair in my voice. If the odds were three-to-two before Lockman had bounced out, now they were two and two-thirds to two.

Dark was the next batter, and as he took his crouching position, his posterior poking out and his whole body twisting and squirming like some impatient and awkward animal straining to get at his prey, I noted on my score-card that Lemon had not got Dark out all day. In the first inning, Dark had .walked. In the third, he had singled on that hit-and-run play upon which the Giants built their two runs. Again in the fourth he had singled.

Dark had been one of the hitting stars (Irvin was the

Monte Irvin, left fielder

other) in the 1951 World Series against the Yankees, and he is the intense type of ball player who performs best when it is most necessary. This is especially so in the field as he was to prove a few minutes later.

Dark has that rare talent of making his errors when they least count. During the 1954 season, I can recall only one error by Dark that was seriously detrimental to the Giants' chances in a ball game, and that was in a game in which the Giants trailed and never scored again. True, the error helped turn a 2-1 ball game into a 5-1 affair, but if the Giants were not going to score anyway, then it would not matter if the error made the score 15-1.

Early in his Giant career, Dark used to terrify the fans and the Giant management by the manner with which he charged bounding balls. Instead of waiting for that nice big hop, body stationed firmly, left leg slightly forward, body turned a bit toward third so that as soon as the ball is brought into the glove, the whole body can twist and move toward first, adding momentum to the throw, Dark used to rush in pellmell, scoop up the grounder on any hop and throw while running toward the plate. It was a dangerous way of making the play—somewhat reminiscent of tennis player Fred Perry returning serve by hitting it on the rising bounce instead of waiting for the ball to reach its full height—and too often Dark would err.

But he soon stopped this senseless charge (though he still rushes the average ball more than any other shortstop) and he stopped making too many errors. Actually, the rush act was a refreshing change from the poised lazy shortstops that cluttered up the National League and who ended every season in states of near collapse. While these athletes were sagging and playing their position "on a dime"—Dark was still full of fire, making his headlong dash at the ball. Because of his astonishing stamina, Dark even then was the best shortstop in his league every September.

At the plate, the Giant captain also fails to paint a picture of athletic grace, and this is surprising because he was a football, track and baseball star at Louisiana State University, and such all-round skill usually makes for a rhythmic performer. Dark seems to have another talent that makes him a star. It is an intangible quality, and though the spectator views it much as you can see smoke coming from the mouth of a smoldering volcano, the real fire is down underneath, unseen.

Ball players on the Giants pay tribute to Dark, but ball players are usually inarticulate souls. They say that Dark is a "take-charge guy," and that is the sum of it. I, for one, wonder how this manifests itself, what he says to his mates, his tone of voice, how he manages to make evident his fighting qualities and leadership.

When Dark and Eddie Stanky, present Cardinal manager, used to play short and second, first for the Boston Braves and then for the Giants (and in each city, a pennant was won), I felt that Stanky was the fire, the sparkplug, and Dark the more talented of the pair.

But when Stanky left for St. Louis, the same seething atmosphere seemed to trail after Dark, and I knew that he was no less the driving force that has helped the Giants in their efforts. Stanky once said, "Dark does so many things so well in the field and at the plate, but it is the things you don't see him do that are the most important."

However this is a negative, and I am still fascinated by the mystery of Alvin Dark. It may be that there is something in his name that has impelled him. Dark. Sometimes he is called Blackie Dark. He uses a black bat, the only ball player I've ever seen using one regularly. He is a man of dark and glowering looks. There is nothing light colored about him, nothing bright or joyous. His is a dark spirit, a raging spirit, the kind that takes losing bitterly and broodingly, and thus, the kind that must win.

That is Alvin Dark, as I imagine him. But to return to the moment at hand, to the second half of the seventh inning of the first World Series contest of 1954, with one man out and the score tied, Dark was just a batter, a dangerous one, and Lemon a pitcher, a skillful, cautious one. And though Alvin gave me the impression that he was about to make another hit, Lemon, pitching in his uncolorful manner, teased him with a bad ball and Dark lunged after it, just as he had in the third inning when he singled. This time he lofted the ball toward the third-base box seats and Al Rosen trotted over and caught it for a simple out.

Dark went back to the dugout, swinging his bat in slashing back-and-forth strokes at the earth at his feet. I imagine he was cursing a blue streak, a midnight blue.

And the phlegmatic Mueller, who gives no impression of "do or die," promptly belted a drive down the right-field line for a single, a ball that was once more stroked with a full-arm swing rather than poked at with the wrists.

Now it was Mays. The odds had dropped to two and one-third to two.

Willie had popped to the shortstop, walked, and grounded to the shortstop, and the crowd sensed that the unleashing of Mays was not far off. There was a stirring, a restive rustling all about me. One does not stop Mays very often. His batting average, when translated into English, means he gets three to four hits in every ten official bats. Today he had no hits in two bats, the walk not included. Certainly a hit in three trips was not asking

96

too much of the lithe young man; it was, in fact, asking only what he had done all season.

And so I said, "Now, Willie, *now*. You're the boy, Willie." Yet I did not mean it.

Mays does not inspire my hopes at the plate as he used to. This is foolish on my part, because he is a far better hitter now than he was when I felt with every swing he'd hit a home run. I cannot help it; I harbor the feeling that Al Lopez is right, that Mays *is* a .270 hitter who might hit .300 with some luck. It was against the rules that he hit more than that in 1954, so undisciplined does he seem.

Sometime around the midseason mark, Mays stopped hitting home runs with any frequency. There was a wild moment or two when it appeared he would certainly hit over fifty home runs and might possibly approach Babe Ruth's record of sixty, that record which my friend Ray Robinson always prefaces with the word "sacrosanct," and which has frightened off every slugger since Ruth.

Every day, it seemed, Mays would come to bat in the second inning and hit the first pitch into the upper left-field stands in the Polo Grounds. After a few days of this, the fans began to *know* that Mays would hit a home run, the way fans knew Ruth would in 1927, the way children expect Santa Claus to have left his trademark when they rise on December 25.

But at the same time that the pitcher finally decided he was no early-season fluke and had to be pitched to more carefully, Mays began to discipline his batting. Actually his disciplining was probably a natural occurrence, a battle for survival and ego-satisfaction.

My daughter who is an infant has learned to push a ball in my direction, because if she doesn't aim true, it will not be pushed back. (I hate getting up from the living

97

room floor once I am comfortably sprawled.) Thus, to keep herself satisfied, she has learned to discipline her ball-pushing.

In a similar way, Mays is fed by base hits; they satisfy him. It is imperative—as in a child—that he be so satisfied. Additionally, he knows his survival in baseball depends upon getting hits. Hence the discipline, occurring a million miles from his everyday consciousness, buried deep somewhere in a tiny fiber of his soul that even he does not know exists.

Mays has a tendency to lunge at a pitched ball (like Clint Hartung or Bobby Thomson), and bad pitches or pitches of less than average speed would often find him off-balance, missing foolishly. So the pitchers began to aim for the outside corner and thereby reduce Mays' ability to hit the ball down the left-field line, and they slowed their pitches to make him provide all the power (a batted ball seems to travel from the bat at a speed in direct ratio to the speed at which it was pitched). But when this happened Mays stopped lunging and started hitting the ball to whatever field seemed called for by the pitch.

Outside pitches were looped into right field (and sometimes into the stands), pitches somewhat to the outside of center were hit into right-center, center, and left-center field, and pitches on the inside (most rare of all, to Mays) were pulled to left field. And as his home-run production slowed down, his base-hit production increased, and with it his batting average until he had won the league title.

The last day of the season, down in Philadelphia, saw Mays facing Robin Roberts, probably as good a pitcher as there exists. At the time Willie was engaged in a struggle for the batting championship with teammate Don Mueller, that mechanical marvel, and Dodger Duke

98

Snider of the liquid grace. Mays hit an inside pitch to left field for a single, and two outside pitches over the head of Richie Ashburn in deep right-center field for a double and a triple.

But as his skill as a batter grows, that first wild and terrifying power seems to have diminished, and there is less thrill in watching him. I speak, of course, for myself. I imagine the pitchers are in no way happier now that Mays has become a .345 batsman.

It was with Mays at the plate in the opening game of the regular season in 1954 that a fond hope of a friend of mine, Dick Kaplan, was realized. Kaplan has always wondered what would happen when a pitch, delivered with blinding speed by a fast-ball pitcher, was hit at precisely the right spot on the bat by a free-swinging slugger, uncoiling on the ball with every once of his power. What would have happened, for instance, had Feller *not* struck out Mize with that blazing fast ball in the All-Star game of 1939, and if instead, Mize had connected perfectly? Where would the ball go, how far, how fast?

Kaplan sat next to me on that opening day in 1954, and watched while Carl Erskine, one of the better fast-ball pitchers, tried to throw a pitch past Mays. Willie hit it with that savage and gorgeous glee he used to bring to the plate. It is too bad he hit it in the Polo Grounds, because a well-hit ball there either will land in the stands, not too far away, or else will clear the roof and disappear. Giant public-relations officials do not chase such balls with a tape measure as do those with the Yankees.

Had Mays hit this Erskine pitch in the Yankee Stadium, it would have been easier to watch, but that still wouldn't have been good enough. What was needed was a completely open flat lot, with markers much like those on a golf driving range.

Mays' blow, that opening day against Erskine, traveled on a blinding blur, a straight line the entire distance until it hit the upper deck above the 414-foot marker. Certainly there was another one hundred and fifty feet left in the drive. More likely it would have gone over six hundred feet in all (yes, it would have, Mickey Mantle) since the ball had shown no disposition to fall from its rising line.

That, however, was the Mays of early 1954. And so I murmured my hopes now but did not trust them. I did not expect to see Willie hit a home run off Lemon, here in the seventh inning of the World Series contest. All I hoped for was a base hit of some size and a rally to stem from it. Mays had been a woefully inept hitter in the 1951 World Series and I hoped he was not going to repeat that record, though the Mays of 1951 and the Mays of 1954 were vastly different players.

But Mays had not solved Lemon as yet, or else Lemon had solved Mays. Willie hit another ground ball to shortstop Strickland who flipped it to Avila, and Mueller was forced for the final out of the seventh.

And now—I thought—they've got two licks apiece. The odds flopped to even money.

NINE

A Giant fan walked by between the seventh and eighth innings and held his fingers in the V-for-Victory sign. I do not know his name; let's just call him Joe. I know he is a Giant fan because I have seen him in the Giant bleachers at every game I have attended. I am not a gregarious person and I do not make friends easily— my inverted snobbism again—so my information about Joe is all second hand. Joe interests me and I wish I could go up to him and chat with him. I can't. But in all the banter at a couple of dozen games, I have learned much— how true it is, I don't know—about Joe. He goes to every Giant game when the Giants are in town, and nearly every Yankee game when the Yankees are in New York (while one team is in New York, the other must be on the road). They tell me that sometimes Joe takes off on the same train the Giants use when they are playing in some out-of-town city, rather than see the Yankees. In any event, he must see a game every day he possibly can.

He knows every ball player, the ball player's wife's first name, how many children they have, what kind of car they drive, where they live. One day I saw Joe leaning over the edge of the bleacher wall, talking to a player. The conversation went something like this:

"How's the migraine, Bob?"

"Lousy."

"Have you tried wet cotton on your eyes? Fifteen minutes at a stretch, every couple of hours or so?"

"Yeah. Tried everything."

"Well," Joe said, "remember me to the wife."

Then the ball player continued onto the field and Joe started to roam the bleachers. He stopped a fan and said, in a confidential manner, yet so that others could hear, "Bob's drinking again," and walked on.

For some reason, Joe incurs dislike. He is a walking fan. That is, he does not claim a seat during the game; so far as I know, no one has ever seen him sitting. He walks back and forth from the right-field section to the left, and up and down, from the railing just above the playing-field level to the highest spot in the bleachers.

He exchanges insults with fans, looking for those standbys who come to Giant games not because they are Giant fans but because they also like to go to games and they have enough left from their unemployment insurance checks to see a few. Joe calls such fans, "bums," and they repay in kind.

Or he walks toward the visiting bullpen and insults the pitchers and catchers sprawled out there. This, of course, is like shooting fish in a barrel. Ball players (with the exception of Ted Williams) take abuse without answering back.

I yelled to Joe, from my anonymity (he had already walked past), "Hey, sit down, you bum." That's what everybody says to Joe.

He waved his hand to indicate he heard, but did not look

Whitey Lockman, first baseman

back. I heard him yell, "This is the inning. The lucky inning."

A chorus of catcalls greeted him, from Giant and Indian fans alike. Nobody cares for Joe. I think it is because he's the child that everybody was and isn't any more, and we hate him for reminding us of how much we have lost. Only Joe remains a child.

I do not know how he supports himself; he is not employed but draws no unemployment check, my bleacher friends tell me. There is a small, growing legend that his family has lots of money and it caters to his desire to remain a child. Joe must be forty years old. So far as I can find out, he *lives* in the Polo Grounds bleachers.

But whereas I dislike Joe, I admit admiration. My major complaint is that I have never seen him watching the ball game. He seems more interested in talking to the visiting bullpen crew. The game itself does not interest him.

But some other Giant rooters I cannot admire. They are that handful of modern fans, found in every ball park, cynical, abusive of the team they allegedly support— cynical of all teams for that matter—and they adhere to the most criminal of all habits of bleacher fans, a habit that is becoming more popular, I'm sorry to say, as the years roll by. They take radios to the game—that portable radio of my wife's mind—and listen to Dodger or Yankee games, their hands held up for silence, while their bodies twist away from the grass in front of them. Sometimes, while sitting in the Polo Grounds bleachers, they even listen to the Giant game!

They are the symbols of the artificial world all about us—the world of substitute values where the substitution is made so glittering and glamorous as to pale the original. They would rather hear a game than see one, or,

104

better still, hear *and* see one at the same time: television. When portable television becomes the rage (grim thought though it may be), they will pack their little sets to the ball parks and glue their eyes to the television screen, quietly cursing the sunlight all around them that is making their reception so dim. Someday we will have ball games played in quiet studios and heavyweight championship prize fights fought before the three officials, the engineers and cameramen and no one else.

Even at this World Series contest, when there is no other game to listen to—and, fortunately, no portable television set to carry—you can spot these portable radio fans. Though the bleachers were packed, you could see them squirming in discomfort, turning around, engaging in wearied chatter while Maglie prepared to pitch to Doby in this, the eighth inning of a tied-up World Series opener. To them, it was so naked and real—adjectiveless, unsoapy. They have grown used to the sensationalism of prize-fight announcers and the screaming enthusiasm of Mel Allen, and to them, the truth of a ball game is dull. They go to the games—they're fans, after all, and it is expected; otherwise they might have to do the dishes or wash the car—and they are bored. Only a 13-12 game makes them a little happy.

I say all this because, right in front of me, two such squirming uneasy men got up as the eighth inning began —not quite three o'clock—and said to all and sundry, "Well, that's enough for *me*." They glared at the rest of us as if we were fools to be sitting here in such a *dull* game. And they went home.

I was stunned. I said to the man on my right, the Cadillac-lover, "Can you imagine that?"

He shook his head in sympathy.

I now had a place for my feet—the bench in front of me—but for two minutes I did not use it. I half expected their return.

They are the people for whom the television screens must grow ever larger; my friend, Don Fine, envisions a future world of tiny people and huge television screens, where everyone gives up his identity, his life, his job, his own family to become part of the drama on the screen—or screens—in front of him. Not even *1984* could conjure so horrible a future.

On the naked, real ball field, grassy and breeze swept and still tingling warm, smelling of sweat and dry wood— Sal Maglie found he had gone as far as he could, and the Indians began to loom as the eventual winners of the first game.

Doby was the batter. In the seventh, Maglie had retired Cleveland in order, and my fear of Doby batting with a man or men on base came to naught. But there was no way of stopping him from batting entirely. He stood there now, swinging his big pale bat, crouched into himself, his body's muscles contracted so they could more furiously uncoil, and Maglie pitched as his tired body dictated.

A fast ball—the last one he was to throw—came blistering toward Doby, and suddenly the crouched, menacing figure had whirled away and into the dirt, the ball whizzing past and against Westrum's glove, to lie innocently on the ground behind the batter. Then Maglie walked him. Doby was the first man Maglie had walked—I was going to say, the first since Al Smith in the first inning, but Smith had been hit on that fourth wild pitch.

When Maglie's control goes in a late inning, he is through. Sometimes he is a bit erratic early in the game, but usually this is a passing matter, under control by the

106

third or fourth inning. But when it occurs late in the game, nothing can be done to remedy the situation. Not even that giant will to triumph can prevail over an arm gone tired and capricious.

Maglie is not Feller of days gone by, a young man who could wind up and throw the ball in the general direction of the plate, knowing that no batter would dare take a toehold against such erratic speed. In those days Feller's lack of control was an added weapon in his arsenal. No, Maglie must throw the ball exactly where he wants to throw it; that is his whole formula.

Now he no longer could.

Liddle and Grissom began to bear down. The call would soon be coming, though I urged, "All right, Sal, let's get two. Slow man up there, Sal, big double-play man. The old d.p., Sal."

Al Rosen was slow, hobbled by injuries at that moment, and the double play was a distinct possibility. Provided Maglie could throw the ball where he wanted to.

He did his best, as he always does.

He threw the twisting curve ball someplace inside, around the fists, but it had little speed and it was not going to drive Rosen off before it broke and clipped the inside corner of the plate. It broke quite slowly—started to, anyway, and Rosen clubbed it, savagely, on the ground into the hole between short and third.

Twice earlier Alvin Dark had gone into that hole, once for a ground ball hit by Rosen himself in the third inning, and again in the fourth for one hit by Strickland. Of the two, Strickland's smash had been the more difficult play, especially because Strickland is the faster man of the two, and because Al Dark never makes any play seem easy. He makes them, nearly all of them, but they never look easy and you always wonder as he scrambles and digs

107

whether he'll get there, whether the throw will be strong enough, true enough, in time.

The play on Strickland in the fourth saw Dark rush into the hole, gather up the ball as he came to a skidding halt, and throw to first, in time by a stride. It was a good, not spectacular play, the kind Dark makes nearly all the time and which shortstops worth their salt must make.

This one was different. The ball was hit harder, nearer to third, and headed for left field.

On such a ball, Dark is another ball player, faster, surer, a player of fury and skill. He ran to his right and angled off a bit from the infield, bent down low like a hound dog in search of the scent of quail, his right hand, the bare hand, darting out.

It is the play of the gambler, of the digger rather than the sure, gliding player of mechanical finesse. Dark's bare-hand stops have often excited me; they seldom result in an out because from that position, running toward short left field, it is impossible for him to turn and make a play to first in time for an out. Sometimes, if there is a terribly slow runner on first, Dark can recover in time to get a force play at second.

But even though he knows that he usually cannot make a play, he continues to thrust his bare hand in front of balls that would otherwise run unimpeded into the outfield. He realizes that sooner or later it will be necessary to knock down such a ball and keep a man from advancing not one base but two—the man from first going to third, or the man on second scoring.

So even when no one is on, Dark goes after such balls with his bare right hand; it is all preparation for the one time he can best use his special skill. There is another reason he must stop the ball. At such a moment it has become a live thing; he must slap it down as you would a fractious animal, lay it at your feet and then stomp on it. It *must* be stopped.

Dark stopped this one, and incidentally won the ball game. For Doby, swift even with his muscular aches, was running with the pitch, and he would have gone on past second, sweeping into third. Later he would have scored. And I would have gone on home downcast. All this, of course, I did not know, nor did Dark as he felt the sting of the baseball against his flesh. Then the ball had burned free of his hand and twisted and rolled away, and he was after it like a shot, picking it up on the grass in short left field. Doby held up at second. Rosen was on first.

Now the game was grinding to its series of climaxes, not like some beautifully constructed play by Shakespeare building to a third-act peak, and then inevitably leveling off in the final fourth and fifth acts, a drama of fifty percent rising action and fifty percent falling. This was a ball game, obeying no rules of the dramatist, building all the time even as it fell.

Here was a high point, punctuated by an abyss. Now was the time for the mind of baseball—the strategy—to assert itself, to stymie muscle for the nonce, and the arena became quiet as that familiar stocky swift waddling figure came from the Giant dugout, Freddie Fitzsimmons, Giant coach, to whom falls the duty of informing the present incumbent of the mound that he is to be replaced.

Fitzsimmons knows what this means, to a pitcher and to a team. He pitched for many long years, most of them for the Giants and then, in his twilight, magnificently for the Dodgers, turning back the clock for a brief while. Fitz threw in a peculiar manner, whirling his back on the batter, facing second base for a moment as he clasped the

109

ball and hid the delivery, and then spinning back to fire his knuckler, the best knuckler I ever saw until Hoyt Wilhelm came along with his magic.

So often did he throw the pitch with a motion not unlike Maglie's, wrenching, short-armed, painful to look at and painful, indeed, for Fitz to throw, so often did he so labor, sweat pouring down his portly frame that finally his arm grew shorter, as though it had rebelled against the torture and tried to shrink into its own shoulder socket.

Fitzsimmons knows the lonely majesty of the man on the mound; no one ever threw with more courage and dignity than this fat man who was so agile that his own fielding ability conspired to defeat him on the greatest day he ever knew. That was in the 1936 World Series, the third game, the Giants and Yankees each having one win. Fitz was pitching a masterpiece, yielding one run when Lou Gehrig hit a tremendous home run into the center-field bleachers in the Yankee Stadium, but giving up nothing else except a few—two or three—little hits. One of the most powerful attacks ever to appear in one uniform—the Yankees of '36, Dickey, DiMaggio, Gehrig, Lazzeri and others—was held in Fitz's sweaty aching palm and by his gnarled red-rubbed knuckles. But the Giants were not hitting either, and so it went, 1-1, until the bottom of the eighth, and a Yankee reached third with two out.

The next man hit a ground ball back to Fitz's left, headed slightly to the second baseman's side of the bag where Burgess Whitehead was gliding over, prepared to make the play for the third out. But Fitz—who yearly made more assists than nearly any pitcher in the National League—went for the ball that by all rights was past him. He managed to flag it down, as Dark was to flag down Rosen's ground ball nearly twenty years later, but the ball spun away and Whitehead, though he changed direction frantically, no longer could make the play and as the ball lay dead on the inner grass, the winning run scampered home.

Later, as some eerie echo, Fitz was to face the Yankees again, while he wore a Dodger uniform, and pitch nearly as well, keeping another vaunted Yankee team in check until his pitching rival, Marius Russo, hit a line drive right back at him. The years had slowed Fitz's great reflexes, but his courage remained the same. He kicked out his leg to stop the ball; the line drive shattered his shin bone, the ball flying fifty feet up into the air, coming down in a fielder's glove for an out. But Fitz was through, and the Yankees went on to win.

Now he was at the mound, on a routine errand, telling Maglie that this time it was he who was through, fiddling on the hill with the tired pitcher until an umpire pushed through the tight little conference and demanded to know of Fitzsimmons who it was to be: Liddle or Grissom. Fitz turned then to the Giant bullpen, stepped clear so that he could be seen, and made a little motion with his left arm as though he were throwing a curve ball. And the umpire broke free of the conference and went running toward the bullpen, waving his left arm.

It was to be Liddle, the left hander.

And in the bullpen, Liddle, obeying the old tradition of all relief hurlers, threw a few more pitches as though he had no idea the umpire was trying to signal him in, to get the game going again, to take the moment out of its stationary abyss and restore it to its high plateau.

The reason why it was Liddle is obvious, I imagine, to anybody who knows anything about baseball. Wertz was a left-handed hitter, Liddle a left-handed pitcher. Through the years it has become a nearly known fact that most

111

left handers do not hit southpaws as well as they do right-handed hurlers. A right-handed pitcher delivers a ball that comes in to a left-handed hitter, his curve ball breaking toward the batter and his bat. A left hander's curve breaks away or else comes steaming in at his body, forcing the left-handed hitter to pull away from the inside pitch, and then sweeping across the plate.

All this is tradition, and as everyone knows, sometimes the tradition fails. Science can explain some of the failures. Some left-handed pitchers throw curves that break *away* from a right-handed hitter. Such pitchers are as effective against right handers as they would be against left handers, probably even more so.

But the left-handed-throwing Liddle does not throw such a curve. His curve breaks in toward right handers' bats, away from left handers'. He is thus more effective against left-handed hitters than against right. Liddle's best pitch is such a curve, delivered with fair speed. It is obvious that he was being brought in to pitch such curves to Wertz, the left-handed hitter who had treated the right-handed Mr. Maglie so rudely. Left handers, it had been reported, were terrible problems to Mr. Wertz, however.

Thus, Liddle.

Liddle is a medium-sized man with a quick, jaunty manner and he throws in quick, jerky movements. He came to New York in the big "unnatural" winter trade that uprooted the Giant hero of 1951, Bob Thomson, and shipped him out to Milwaukee in return for pitcher John Antonelli. Other players were also involved, including a man with the improbable name of Ebba St. Claire, whom Leo Durocher referred to warmly as his number-one catcher when the 1954 season began. St. Claire spent the last half

112

of the season with the Giants' farm team in the American Association.

Liddle finally saw the umpire and gathered up his jacket and walked toward the mound with a pleasantly cocky step as though this bit of business ought not to take too long or be too arduous. He had warmed up, off and on, since the very first inning, since the sixth pitch of the game in fact, and he had taken those extra few warmup tosses only because tradition demands that a bullpen pitcher must make the umpire run as far out as possible before he accepts the call to duty.

So Liddle was warmed up sufficiently, and I yelled a friendly word to him as he stepped briskly along, and then I turned and watched Maglie.

He stood on the mound, useless now, waiting for Liddle to arrive before he set off across the diamond and to the clubhouse. He had given up the ball to Fitzsimmons and had moved slightly away from the high point of the hill, off on the sloping ground as though unconsciously he knew his role was over, his place of command usurped by this snappy compact man who now reached the center of the diamond, swapped his jacket for the ball and started his practice throws to catcher Westrum.

And while Liddle wheeled them in, swift and neat and altogether left-handed, Maglie walked past second base and out toward us in the bleachers. There was a sprinkling of applause for the man who had come into the stadium some time before eleven o'clock that morning, clean shaven and tastefully dressed, and was now going off tired and grimy, his face coated with sweat and dark beard.

The applause grew as he neared the bleachers; we appreciated what he had tried to do, what he had done in fact, keeping the Indians off while the Giants battled even, and if, in the last analysis, he had failed, why then, he had failed nobly. All the great people and great things in life are failures; it is in doing what we cannot do but must try to do that humans rise to their exalted fulfillment. Maglie had tried to do with an old man's arm and back what a young man might not even have been able to do as well—of such failures is greatness made.

So the applause became swollen and Maglie tried to raise his head to acknowledge it, but he was too tired and probably too bitter, so all we saw was the little sheepish wave of the hand, the same wave with which he had greeted us in the morning, an echo twisted out of shape.

It was not all applause, of course. The woman in the red hat who had threatened Maglie with an early shower, now boasted of her prognosticating ability. "I told you so, Sal," she said, shaking her fist at him, "I told you so, you bum."

Leaping to my feet I shouted, "That's all right, Sal, we'll get 'em for you. Don't worry, Sal."

His only response was the scrape of his spiked shoes as they went up the stairs to the dressing room. Then he disappeared.

TEN

And like wolves drawn to our fresh prey, we had already forgotten him, eyes riveted on Liddle, while off to the side of the plate Vic Wertz studied the new Giant pitcher and made whatever estimations he had to make.

Wertz had hit three times already; nobody expected more of him. He had hit one of Maglie's fast balls in the first inning, a pitch that was headed for the outside corner but Wertz's bat was too swift and he had pulled the ball for a triple. Then he hit a little curve, a dinky affair that was either Maglie's slider or a curve that didn't break too well, and drove it into left field for a single. Finally, he had pulled another outside pitch that—by all rights—he shouldn't have been able to pull, so far from the right-field side of the plate was it. But he had pulled it, as great sluggers will pull any ball because that is how home runs are made. Wertz hadn't hit a home run on that waist-high pitch on the outside; he had rifled it to right field for another single.

But that was all off Maglie, forgotten behind a door over five hundred feet from the plate. Now it was Liddle, jerking into motion as Wertz poised at the plate, and then the motion smoothed out and the ball came sweeping in to Wertz, a shoulder-high pitch, a fast ball that probably would have been a fast curve, except that Wertz was coming around and hitting it, hitting it about as hard as I have ever seen a ball hit, on a high line to dead center field.

For whatever it is worth, I have seen such hitters as Babe Ruth, Lou Gehrig, Ted Williams, Jimmy Foxx, Ralph Kiner, Hack Wilson, Johnny Mize, and lesser-known but equally long hitters as Wally Berger and Bob Seeds send the batted ball tremendous distances. None, that I recall, ever hit a ball any harder than this one by Wertz in my presence.

And yet I was not immediately perturbed. I have been a Giant fan for years, twenty-eight years to be exact, and I have seen balls hit with violence to extreme center field which were caught easily by Mays, or Thomson before him, or Lockman or Ripple or Hank Leiber or George Kiddo Davis, that most marvelous fly catcher.

I did not—then—feel alarm, though the crack was loud and clear, and the crowd's roar rumbled behind it like growing thunder. It may be that I did not believe the ball would carry as far as it did, hard hit as it was. I have seen hard-hit balls go a hundred feet into an infielder's waiting glove, and all that one remembers is crack, blur, spank. This ball did not alarm me because it was hit to dead center field—Mays' territory—and not between the fielders, into those dread alleys in left-center and right-center which lead to the bullpens.

And this was not a terribly high drive. It was a long low fly or a high liner, whichever you wish. This ball was hit not nearly so high as the triple Wertz struck earlier in

116

Photo: New York Daily News

the day, so I may have assumed that it would soon start to break and dip and come down to Mays, not too far from his normal position.

Then I looked at Willie, and alarm raced through me, peril flaring against my heart. To my utter astonishment, the young Giant center fielder—the inimitable Mays, most skilled of outfielders, unique for his ability to scent the length and direction of any drive and then turn and move to the final destination of the ball—Mays was turned full around, head down, running as hard as he could, straight toward the runway between the two bleacher sections.

I knew then that I had underestimated—badly underestimated—the length of Wertz's blow.

I wrenched my eyes from Mays and took another look at the ball, winging its way along, undipping, unbreaking, forty feet higher than Mays' head, rushing along like a locomotive, nearing Mays, and I thought then: it will beat him to the wall.

Through the years I have tried to do what Red Barber has cautioned me and millions of admiring fans to do: take your eye from the ball after it's been hit and look at the outfielder and the runners. This is a terribly difficult thing to learn; for twenty-five years I was unable to do it. Then I started to take stabs at the fielder and the ball, alternately. Now I do it pretty well. Barber's advice pays off a thousand times in appreciation of what is unfolding, of what takes some six or seven seconds—that's all, six or seven seconds—and of what I can see in several takes, like a jerking motion picture, until I have enough pieces to make nearly a whole.

There is no perfect whole, of course, to a play in baseball. If there was, it would require a God to take it all in. For instance, on such a play, I would like to know what

118

Manager Durocher is doing—leaping to the outer lip of the sunken dugout, bent forward, frozen in anxious fear? And Lopez—is he also frozen, hope high but too anxious to let it swarm through him? The coaches—have they started to wave their arms in joy, getting the runners moving, or are they half-waiting, in fear of the impossible catch and the mad scramble that might ensue on the base paths?

The players—what have they done? The fans—are they standing, or half-crouched, yelling (I hear them, but since I do not see them, I do not know who makes that noise, which of them yells and which is silent)? Has activity stopped in the Giant bullpen where Grissom still had been toiling? Was he now turned to watch the flight of the ball, the churning dash of Mays?

No man can get the entire picture; I did what I could, and it was painful to rip my sight from one scene frozen forever on my mind, to the next, and then to the next.

I had seen the ball hit, its rise; I had seen Mays' first backward sprint; I had again seen the ball and Mays at the same time, Mays still leading. Now I turned to the diamond —how long does it take the eyes to sweep and focus and telegraph to the brain?—and there was the vacant spot on the hill (how often we see what is not there before we see what is there) where Liddle had been and I saw him at the third-base line, between home and third (the wrong place for a pitcher on such a play; he should be behind third to cover a play there, or behind home to back up a play there, but not in between).

I saw Doby, too, hesitating, the only man, I think, on the diamond who now conceded that Mays might catch the ball. Doby is a center fielder and a fine one and very fast himself, so he knows what a center fielder can do. He must have gone nearly halfway to third, now he was coming

119

back to second base a bit. Of course, he may have known that he could jog home if the ball landed over Mays' head, so there was no need to get too far down the line.

Rosen was as near to second as Doby, it seemed. He had come down from first, and for a second—no, not that long, nowhere near that long, for a hundred-thousandth of a second, more likely—I thought Doby and Rosen were Dark and Williams hovering around second, making some foolish double play on this ball that had been hit three hundred and thirty feet past them. Then my mind cleared; they were in Cleveland uniforms, not Giant, they were Doby and Rosen.

And that is all I allowed my eyes on the inner diamond. Back now to Mays—had three seconds elapsed from the first ominous connection of bat and ball?—and I saw Mays do something that he seldom does and that is so often fatal to outfielders. For the briefest piece of time—I cannot shatter and compute fractions of seconds like some atom gun—Mays started to raise his head and turn it to his left, as though he were about to look behind him.

Then he thought better of it, and continued the swift race with the ball that hovered quite close to him now, thirty feet high and coming down (yes, finally coming down) and again—for the second time—I knew Mays would make the catch.

In the Polo Grounds, there are two square-ish green screens, flanking the runway between the two bleacher sections, one to the left-field side of the runway, the other to the right. The screens are intended to provide a solid dark background for the pitched ball as it comes in to the batter. Otherwise he would be trying to pick out the ball from a far-off sea of shirts of many colors, jackets, balloons, and banners.

Wertz's drive, I could see now, was not going to end

120

up in the runway on the fly; it was headed for the screen on the right-field side.

The fly, therefore, was not the longest ball ever hit in the Polo Grounds, not by a comfortable margin. Wally Berger had hit a ball over the left-field roof around the four-hundred foot marker. Joe Adcock had hit a ball into the center-field bleachers. A Giant pitcher, Hal Schumacher, had once hit a ball over the left-field roof, about as far out as Berger's. Nor—if Mays caught it—would it be the longest ball ever caught in the Polo Grounds. In either the 1936 or 1937 World Series—I do not recall which—Joe DiMaggio and Hank Leiber traded gigantic smashes to the foot of the stairs within that runway; each man had caught the other's. When DiMaggio caught Leiber's, in fact, it meant the final out of the game. DiMaggio caught the ball and barely broke step to go up the stairs and out of sight before the crowd was fully aware of what had happened.

So Mays' catch—if he made it—would not necessarily be in the realm of the improbable. Others had done feats that bore some resemblance to this.

Yet Mays' catch—if, indeed, he was to make it—would dwarf all the others for the simple reason that he, too, could have caught Leiber's or DiMaggio's fly, whereas neither could have caught Wertz's. Those balls had been towering drives, hit so high the outfielder could run forever before the ball came down. Wertz had hit his ball harder and on a lower trajectory. Leiber—not a fast man—was nearing second base when DiMaggio caught his ball; Wertz—also not fast—was at first when . . .

When Mays simply slowed down to avoid running into the wall, put his hands up in cup-like fashion over his left shoulder, and caught the ball much like a football player catching leading passes in the end zone.

He had turned so quickly, and run so fast and truly that he made this impossible catch look—to us in the bleachers —quite ordinary. To those reporters in the press box, nearly six hundred feet from the bleacher wall, it must have appeared far more astonishing, watching Mays run and run until he had become the size of a pigmy and then he had run some more, while the ball diminished to a mote of white dust and finally disappeared in the dark blob that was Mays' mitt.

The play was not finished, with the catch.

Now another pet theory of mine could be put to the test. For years I have criticized baserunners who advance from second base while a long fly ball is in the air, then return to the base once the catch has been made and proceed to third after tagging up. I have wondered why these men have not held their base; if the ball is not caught, they can score from second. If it is, surely they will reach third. And—if they are swift—should they not be able to score from second on enormously long flies to dead center field?

Here was such a fly; here was Doby so close to second before the catch that he must have practically been touching the bag when Mays was first touching the drive, his back to the diamond. Now Doby could—if he dared—test the theory.

And immediately I saw how foolish my theory was when the thrower was Mays.

It is here that Mays outshines all others. I do not think the catch made was as sensational as some others I have seen, although no one else could have made it. I recall a catch made by Fred Lindstrom, a converted third baseman who had bad legs, against Pittsburgh. Lindstrom ran to the right-center field wall beyond the Giants' bullpen and leaped high to snare the ball with his gloved hand. Then

122

his body smashed into the wall and he fell on his back, his gloved hand held over his body, the speck of white still showing. After a few seconds, he got to his feet, quite groggy, but still holding the ball. That was the finest catch I can recall, and the account of the game in next day's New York *Herald-Tribune* indicated it might have been the greatest catch ever made in the Polo Grounds.

Yet Lindstrom could not have reached the ball Wertz hit and Mays would have been standing at the wall, ready to leap and catch the ball Lindstrom grabbed.

Mays never left his feet for the ball Wertz hit; all he did was outrun the ball. I do not diminish the feat; no other center fielder that I have ever seen (Joe and Dom DiMaggio, Terry Moore, Sammy West, Eddie Roush, Earle Combs, and Duke Snider are but a few that stand out) could have done it for no one else was as fast in getting to the ball. But I am of the opinion that had not Mays made that slight movement with his head as though he were going to look back in the middle of flight, he would have caught the ball standing still.

The throw to second base was something else again.

Mays caught the ball, and then whirled and threw, like some olden statue of a Greek javelin hurler, his head twisted away to the left as his right arm swept out and around. But Mays is no classic study for the simple reason that at the peak of his activity, his baseball cap flies off. And as he turned, or as he threw—I could not tell which, the two motions were welded into one—off came the cap, and then Mays himself continued to spin around after the gigantic effort of returning the ball whence it came, and he went down flat on his belly, and out of sight.

But the throw! What an astonishing throw, to make all other throws ever before it, even those four Mays himself had made during fielding practice, appear the

123

flings of teen-age girls. This was the throw of a giant, the throw of a howitzer made human, arriving at second base—to Williams or Dark, I don't know which, but probably Williams, my memory says Dark was at the edge of the outfield grass, in deep shortstop position—just as Doby was pulling into third, and as Rosen was scampering back to first.

I wonder what will happen to Mays in the next few years. He may gain in finesse and batting wisdom, but he cannot really improve much because his finest talent lies in his reflex action. He is so swift in his reflexes, the way young Joe Louis was with his hands when, cobra-like, they would flash through the thinnest slit in a foe's defense, Louis, lashing Paulino Uzcudun with the first hard punch he threw, drilled into the tiniest opening and crushing the man who had never before been knocked out. That is Mays, too. Making a great catch and whirling and throwing, before another man would have been twenty feet from the ball.

And until those reflexes slow down, Mays must be regarded as off by himself, not merely *a* great ball player, but *the* great ball player of our time.

(I am not discussing his hitting here; for some strange reason—National League-itis, I guess—when I discuss the native ability of a ball player, I invariably narrow my gaze to his defensive ability. DiMaggio was a better hitter in his prime than Mays is now, maybe than Mays ever will be, although no hitter was ever as good as Mays at the same stage of their respective careers—check Ruth, Wagner, Cobb, Hornsby in their second full year of play and you will see what I mean.)

Still, Willie's 1954 season at the plate may have been some freak occurrence. It happens sometimes that a ball player hits all season far above his norm. I am thinking

124

of Ferris Fain who led the league a few years ago, though he had never been an impressive hitter before. My wife inquired about this man Fain, of whom she was suddenly hearing so much. I told her that he was a pretty good ball player, an excellent defensive first baseman, and a fair hitter. She said, "Fair? He's leading the league, isn't he?"

I said, "Yes, but that's a fluke. He's hitting way over his head. Watch what happens next year." *

Or take Carl Furillo hitting over .340 in 1953. Furillo is a fine hitter, a solid .300 hitter who can drive in nearly a hundred runs a season, but .340 is not his normal average. Possibly .345 is nowhere near Mays' norm; nothing in the past had indicated he could hit that high.

I do not list Mays among the great hitters, though I concede that one day we all may. As a fielder, he is already supreme.

So much for Mays and the catch.

* The following year Fain led the league again.

ELEVEN

The final rumble of the crowd's roar had rolled away, trailing off over the top of the grandstand and into the fine blue sky. The shadow of the stadium now covered the plate and first base and all of right field; it had started to bend toward the pitcher's box as the sun edged nearer first base, hanging over the lip of the roof. The flags on the right-field side were swept out nearly straight, while those on the left-field side hung in soft billowing ripples. (I do not explain this; I merely report it; it is so.)

And on the field itself, the catch had done no more than stop an apparently inexorable Indian attack; it had not wiped it out. There was Doby on third, Rosen on first. One man was out, and again the mind took over, the wheels of reason churning furiously. Liddle had thrown his one pitch and got his man out (isn't that the way it will seem to some fan in the year 2001 as he peers through the dust covering the box score?) and now he himself was out.

Lopez had sent in Hank Majeski, a veteran utility infielder, thirty-eight years old, the oldest man on either roster, with fifteen years in the major leagues, so many of them with lowly ball clubs like the Philadelphia Athletics that Majeski must have long ago despaired of ever seeing such a day as this.

But here he was now, called on to hit for Dave Philley, because Majeski is right handed, and Philley, though listed in the program as hitting either right or left, is most effective left handed. Pitcher Liddle, still in the game, had not changed any (though he might have aged considerably); he was left-handed. (You would think that Wertz had knocked galley-west all that silliness about right handers and left handers.)

Durocher now felt the challenge. All afternoon long he had allowed his men to flex their muscles, run, hit, throw and err—entirely on their own, except for the hit-and-run play in the third inning with which the Giants tied the score. But a Durocher on the sidelines for more than two hours is a man in torment; he has to start thinking, too. So out came Liddle, in came right-handed Grissom to face right-handed Majeski.

Liddle walked from the mound, with the same jaunty manner as before, and the fans jeered him good-naturedly. The crowd was now making noise at every motion on the diamond, the appearance of new batters, new pitchers, the clustering conferences at the plate and on the infield—a great frenzied noisy throng now, no longer merely a restive, whooshing one.

The mental activity was not yet over. Lopez was in the commanding position because a pitcher brought into a game must face at least one man—Liddle had done this, but Grissom had not, so Durocher would have to use Grissom no matter who batted for the Indians. This left

127

Lopez one more strategic move. He yanked Majeski—after those fifteen long years—and put in Dale Mitchell, not a long-ball hitter, but quite skilled at hitting line drives to left field, à la Don Mueller. Mitchell, needless to say, is left handed.

And that is how it ended up, Mitchell versus Grissom.

On the face of it, Lopez won the battle. He had started the changes and he had finished them. And yet what it amounted to was a choice of Liddle against Majeski, or Grissom against Mitchell, for Durocher knew, sure as beans, that as soon as he called in Grissom, Lopez would call out Majeski and replace him with Mitchell. And I think Durocher came out on top, even though Mitchell is a better hitter than Majeski. Grissom was the key man; in him, Durocher had one of the finest relief pitchers in baseball, a man more certain to stop dead that Indian attack than was Liddle, more certain, probably, than anyone else on the Giants with the possible exception of Wilhelm.

Grissom is another oldtimer, nearly as old as Maglie who is nearly as old as Majeski. Maglie once said about Marv Grissom, "I'll win twenty games if Grissom's arm holds up." Though my wife thought this was a very funny remark when she read it in the paper, I recall that many pitchers have said it about their relief pitchers. Lefty Gomez said it about himself and Johnny Murphy many years ago, and there is an unsubstantiated rumor that Lincoln said it about Grant in '65.

Grissom himself probably said it about one of his relievers when he was an overpowering pitcher for the Chicago White Sox a few years back. At that time he got by with a blazing fast ball, but lately he has come to develop the screwball as his best pitch. The screwball is the answer to the problem of right-handed pitchers

128

Vic Wertz, first baseman

versus left-handed hitters; it is a curve that breaks in opposite fashion to the normal curve. As delivered by a right hander like Grissom, it curves *away* from a left hander such as Mitchell. So more and more, it appeared that Durocher had triumphed: not only is Grissom a capable performer in a tight situation, but he is as effective against left-handed hitters as he is against right.

A word here about the screwball. It is today enjoying a renaissance, just as a few years ago the knuckle ball did. Carl Hubbell, of course, was the prime advocate of the screwball (if we forget the fadeaway—a much better word for the same pitch—that Christy Mathewson threw twenty years before Hub). Hubbell used the pitch so often and for so many years, twisting his whole left arm in an unnatural clockwise direction, that today his arm hangs in such a manner that his left palm points out and to the rear when he walks along.

Hubbell had been warned in his early pitching history as a tryout hurler for the Detroit Tigers to forego this delivery; they said it would put such a strain on his arm that his career would be seriously curtailed. Hubbell lasted sixteen years with the Giants, winning two hundred and fifty-three games, and four World Series contests.

Grissom, however, had no such worry. He did not discover the screwball until he was nearly thirty-six years old. He had used it more and more often during the past season because that erstwhile pitch, his fast ball, has deserted him, as it must desert all of us. Grissom also credits his return to form to vitamin-B injections that he took late in the season, a cheering note in dark contrast to the cigars that Sal Maglie smokes and the whisky that Dusty Rhodes reputedly drinks. In this day and age of disillusion it is refreshing to have one's faith restored in the great clean-cut American way of life.

130

Thus refreshed and cleansed, I felt quite confident as the tall lean Grissom stepped in to face Mitchell. I looked forward to this battle, after so deliberate a stage setting.

Grissom walked Mitchell on four pitches.

The wheels ground again.

George Strickland was the next Indian batter, one of the men who make up that bottom of the Cleveland order, a man whose broken jaw in 1954 kept him out of the lineup so long that, once back in, he was not able to find his batting eye. Not that his eye had ever been too sharp. Strickland is one of those good-field, no-hit shortstops of which baseball today has so many. His broken jaw hurt him in other ways as well. Unable to eat solid foods, Strickland lost weight and thereby reduced his strength and power.

Thus far today he had struck out, grounded out and popped out. Now Lopez retired him to the sidelines while Dave Pope, a utility outfielder and—once more—a left-handed batter, entered the box. Pope is a compactly built young man, put together somewhat like Don Liddle, and a relative newcomer to major-league baseball. Certainly this was the most important moment of his athletic life—the bases now loaded, the score tied, and one man out in the first half of the eighth inning. All Pope had to do was hit a long fly (though with Mays throwing the way he was, he had better not hit it to center), or a ground ball that would not result in a double play or an out at the plate.

Instead, Grissom struck him out, on a pitch that seemed to this observer—sitting over five hundred feet from home plate—a trifle high. The crowd exploded, and I made no audible protest over the third-strike call. This was the big out, the second out, and now a base hit would be necessary for a Cleveland run, unless Grissom walked the

131

next man, hit him, wild pitched, balked, or unless the Giant defense erred, or unless the Cleveland runner on third stole home. None of these is impossible, but each is unlikely, especially the last. It is doubtful that any recent major-league club ever came into a series with as little speed or daring as the Indians brought along in 1954.

Their batter was the catcher, Jim Hegan, a big fellow who is more renowned as a receiver of pitched balls than a hitter of them, although he is by no means a hopeless man with a bat.

As he proved a moment later, coming within inches of hitting a grand-slam home run.

He hit a fly ball that headed into left field. The Polo Grounds left field is further removed from home plate than right field (though it is still ridiculously close), but the upper deck juts out so that fly balls, on their way downward toward a left fielder's waiting glove, have a nasty habit of grazing the upper deck overhang and falling onto the grass for a home run.

For a moment, Hegan's fly seemed to be just such a ball. Left fielder Irvin had edged as close to the fence as was possible—usually a sure sign that the ball will either land in the upper deck or strike the facing at the base of the upper deck. At least a dozen times I have seen this happen—the left fielder pressed against the fence as though he hoped to push back the stands to make more room for the lazily dropping fly ball, and then the gentle smiting of the façade and the ball lying innocently at the feet of the left fielder, while the batter runs around the bases, sometimes hesitating at second base as though not sure he had actually hit a home run.

But then—that lovely law of averages, most divine of all ordinances!—Irvin suddenly stepped away from the fence to gather in the ball. The little breeze—so soft for so long—had developed backbone, and Hegan's fly ball was ever so slightly pushed by it, away from the beckoning overhang.

Again the crowd roared, not the whooshing sigh but a resounding noise of approval. In re-checking my scorecard for that half-inning, I see that the Indians, with any sort of luck, would have had five runs, with less luck, four. With no luck, they got no runs, and the 2-2 game went rushing toward its final climaxes.

TWELVE

Once reprieved, it next became the Giants' turn to threaten. Lemon began the inning as did Maglie, walking the first man he faced, Henry Thompson. The Giants played for one run, knowing that one run at this stage would probably win. Monte Irvin, hitless all day, bunted in front of the plate, and Hegan darted out to throw to Wertz, as Thompson moved to second.

Here was the leading run in scoring position, with little Davey at the plate and Westrum to follow. Lemon threw his down-curve in on Williams' hands and the second baseman hit it sharply to Al Rosen's left. The Indian third baseman moved well on this play, snatching up the ball and firing it to first, just ahead of the running Williams. And because the play was in front of Rosen, Thompson was forced to stay on second. Had Williams hit his ground ball to Avila or to Wertz, the defense would have been forced to pay full heed to Williams, allowing Thompson to reach third.

I present this small "if" for whatever it is worth; I think

it is worth much—and little. I have never seen a second baseman pick up a ground ball in his regular fielding depth and be able to throw out a runner going from second to third. Rabbit Maranville went over twenty years, to the very last day of his regular season in the National League, before he saw such a play made. For a first baseman, it is even more difficult unless he is playing in close for a possible bunt and the ball is instead rapped straight at him.

So Lemon's control—off for a moment when he walked Thompson—was vitally true here. Had his pitch not caught that inside corner, Williams might have succeeded in hitting to the right side, and Thompson would have gone to third.

And when Lemon threw a wild pitch to the next man— Wes Westrum—Thompson, who took third, would have scored instead.

That is the much of the "if."

The littleness of it is simply that it did not occur, just as a thousand other things did not occur. Williams hit to Rosen, *not* to Avila. Thompson anchored at second. And on the wild pitch he moved to third. The score remained 2-2.

And with Westrum up, I was now positive Lemon would handle the Giant catcher with contemptuous ease. Wes had two hits and a savage line drive to Doby. That was enough for me. I would wait for the ninth for the Giant victory.

But Westrum, whose batting slump had extended five years, had not had enough. He hit the ball hard again, another blistering line drive, and again he hit it right at Doby. A few feet to either side—well, enough of these ifs.

The game entered the ninth inning, the clock rushing well past three. I had been in the bleachers for nearly six hours and I was tired, hungry and painfully stiff from sitting my plank so long. I had subsisted on two hot dogs, one beer and two cigars. That wind rustling the flags on the right-field side of the diamond was something we could see, but did not feel. A little wind, in fact, would have been most welcome. When I took my seat at ten that morning, there had been a bit of tang to the air, and the hot-coffee salesmen did a bustling business. But by eleven, the coffee hawkers had disappeared, their places being taken by the beer and soda-pop boys. The weather had become quite hot, near or over eighty, it seemed, and I had long ago taken off my jacket, sitting there in my shirtsleeves.

The ninth inning was all Irvin, and I suffered with him. Lemon was the first Indian hitter, and the fans applauded him, as they had done in the seventh inning, except this time they were noisier in their approbation. I again joined in, and then I yelled to Grissom, "All right, Marv, strike this bum out."

Grissom did not strike him out; he induced Lemon to hit a lazy fly ball to Irvin who easily caught it. Al Smith did the same thing, and Irvin came running in to catch this one also, although he seemed to have a bit of trouble with the ball. The sun might have been in Irvin's eyes; his shadow stretched directly behind him as he charged the ball.

The fan behind me—who had delighted in Irvin's discomfiture a few innings back on another fly ball—now repeated his remark about Irvin's eyesight, and I said, "He caught it, that's all that counts. He gets 'em all. Don't worry about Irvin."

The man was quiet, and a minute later I was the biggest damn fool in the park. For Avila hit a third fly to Irvin, looping out to short left field, and Irvin came running in,

136

Don Mueller, right fielder

glove in front of him, and at the precise moment that he reached for the ball I knew he was going to drop it. There was an air of uncertainty about Irvin and it swept to the fans. They made a sucking breath and an *ooh* sound a split-second before the ball hit Irvin's glove and bounced off in front of him.

Irvin tried too hard to redeem the play on the spot. He and Dark had the ball surrounded as it bounded to the grass and up again, about three feet high. Irvin grabbed at the ball, switched it from glove to bare hand, and threw before he had regained full control of his bent-forward lunging body. The result was a throw without any real zip, into second base well after Avila had arrived there.

The man behind me chortled and said, "Oh, yeah, sure. He gets 'em all, all right. Oh, yeah. Sure he does. Oh, yeah."

I tried to shrivel away and shrug it off, but the woman in the red hat turned and said, "How do you like *that*, Mister Giant Fan?"

Now I was stung. "I like it fine, Brooklyn," I said. "Those bums couldn't score if we dropped eighteen fly balls. Watch Doby strike out."

She bent toward me and said, "Yeah, he'll strike out, all right. He'll hit it where he lives."

This time I *had* to tell her. I said, "Doby lives in Paterson. That's over there." I waved my hand toward the plate.

She said, "Nnahhh. That's all *you* know. He lives over there." She pointed past the bleacher section and in the general direction of the Harlem River and England.

I gave up and she turned around and sat down.

Doby didn't hit it to Paterson or England. As Maglie had done in the inning previous, Grissom worked too carefully on the strong slugger and walked him. If the pattern of the eighth inning were to be repeated here, Rosen would now hit, and Wertz would come up.

Rosen instead, hit another fly at the tortured Irvin (the last man in the eighth had flied out to Irvin; the first three men in the ninth had hit flies to him) and Monte once more ran in a little and had trouble locating it, and then caught it.

I yelled, nearly entirely hoarse by this time, "That's the way, Monte, that's grabbing the big one."

The man behind me was silent. For he knew that with the third Indian out in the ninth, the odds had swung heavily to the Giants. Any run they scored now would win the game, whereas a run in the eighth would only have put them ahead. This was the equivalent of a hockey game's overtime period of "sudden death." It would not remain so once the Giants made out, but every time the Giants batted with the score still tied, sudden death would prevail. That was the way I liked it.

Grissom stepped in against Lemon, and the crowd hailed the reliefer, who quickly struck out. Lockman did no better, hitting a sickly grounder back to Lemon who threw to big Wertz, and there were two outs.

Then with two out in the last half of the ninth inning of this tied game, Dark hit a long fly in the same general direction as Hegan's of an inning and a half ago. This ball, however, was much harder and longer hit, and this time it seemed certain that the ball would hit the overhang.

I yelled, what I hoped would be my last serious yell, "That's it, that's it. All the way," waving my left arm as if to propel some air in the direction of the ball and give it the necessary momentum to make the stands. But once more, in this game full of echoes, the left fielder edged to the fence, looking up hopelessly and helplessly, and then stepping away nimbly to make the catch a stride from the wall.

The ball had been hit nearly four hundred feet, but it meant no more than another out, the last out of the ninth inning. Still, I had had a little boost. It seemed that the innings were finally taking their toll on Lemon, even though he still appeared indefatigable, so smoothly was he throwing the ball and so accurately. The down-curve was breaking around the knees, picking up the outside corner, and he had pitched magnificently from the fifth inning on.

Yet Dark's ball had been well hit. I would not let my confidence be shaken at this stage.

THIRTEEN

The tenth inning paraded in. It would have to be the last one—I thought with grim amusement—my scorecard goes no further. And, I had made so many changes in the eighth inning that I was running out of room. For instance, the sixth Cleveland spot on my batting order now read, Philley, r.f., Majeski (8), Mitchell (8), Dente s.s. (8). The 8s referred to the inning in which these gentlemen made their initial appearance. To squeeze Dente in, I had to use the margin. Any more changes in the sixth spot would mean a name written either at the top or bottom of the page, rather than on that sixth line provided on the program.

And so I resolved that the tenth be the last inning.

Vic Wertz had the same general idea.

To open the tenth, he made his fourth hit, a double between Irvin and Mays that the center fielder picked up and threw into third base on the fly. As soon as that ball was hit, it was plainly headed for the open space between the two fielders. Mays was, in the parlance of the radio announcers, "shading" Wertz a bit toward right field. Irvin, as is the habit of "opposite" fielders—that is, left fielders on men who usually hit to right, or right fielders on men who usually hit to left—was crowding in toward the diamond, a few steps toward the left-field foul line. So the ball, though hit higher and not as far as the eighth-inning drive, was completely unplayable. In fact, Irvin seemed merely to jog after it, conceding two things: one, that the ball would land uncaught, and, two, that Mays would get there first anyway.

So Mays, rushing over from his post in center field, took the ball on the run with his bare hand, shouting Irvin off and gesturing with his left hand so that they would not run into each other. Then he whirled and threw to third base.

Not *toward* third base. To it. He did not lose his cap, nor did he fall down, despite the twisting, flashing move. The ball traveled directly to Henry Thompson who caught it standing one stride in front of the base. Wertz made no attempt to stretch his hit, though a faster man would have bluffed a dash from second.

No one could blame Wertz, though. He and the Indians had seen Mays make those four throws in fielding practice (I'm sure the Indians watched, even if only a few hundred fans did), and they had seen his fantastic throw from the bleacher screen in the eighth inning. Wertz had no intention of moving from second, and if a much faster man had made his dash for third and continued running, he would have been out for sure.

A little shiver went through me when Mays threw that ball to Thompson. Here was the final climaxing of an exhibition of power, speed and accuracy that must be unequaled in any sport. Mays took that last base hit as it bounded toward the junction of the left-field stands and

142

Photo: TCMA

Dusty Rhodes (center)

the bleachers, some thirty feet short of that junction. He was running full speed toward the left-field bullpen. He had to bend and scoop up the ball before he threw. Yet he got rid of the ball more quickly this time than he had in the eighth inning and though the throw might not have been as long (by about five feet), it came with more speed and on a slightly lower trajectory all the way to Thompson's glove.

At this point, I think, the Indians quit. It is not fair to say they quit in the eighth when Mays made his catch. They still had clawed away, stopping the Giants in the eighth and ninth, and they had opened the tenth (or at least Wertz had) full of vinegar. But when Mays again indicated he was not Mays, but Superman—they must have known they were through.

I do not say this in any derogatory sense. It just is that the sense of the inevitable now slowly stole over the arena. The feeling—foolish, I know, yet terribly sound— was that nothing the Indians did would matter—no matter how far they hit the ball or how well Lemon pitched. Fate had decided (with the help of a young man in center field) and once having writ, all that remained was the runs, hits and errors.

The Indians bravely went through the motions. Wertz had done his bit nobly. No longer was he needed. He had made his fourth hit and now he could take himself and his flapping shin protector to a place of well-earned rest. Probably he was delighted; he had already seen too much of Willie Mays.

Rudy Regalado, that spring sensation who had threatened to break into the Cleveland starting lineup back in March of 1954 and had since found his way into games usually only when a pinch runner was needed, now came out of the Indian dugout to run for Wertz at second, and the Indian slugger received a burst of cheering.

No doubt many of those cheering were Giant fans who were as equally delighted to see Wertz leave.

Sam Dente—who had gone in to play shortstop in the eighth inning after Strickland had been taken out for Dave Pope—came to bat. Dente was batting in the sixth place even though Strickland had been hitting seventh, because Pope had stayed in the game after he had hit for the regular shortstop.

Dente did what was asked of him; he sacrificed himself so that Regalado might reach third base, bunting the ball toward third, bringing Henry Thompson away from his bag to make the pickup and throw to first. Regalado moved to the undefended base.

On the face of it, the Indians had an extreme threat poised over the Giants' heads. The woman in the red hat —unwilling to read the handwriting on the wall, or unable—got up and howled, "All right, Pope, hit it where you live."

My lips curled in silent scorn. A Dodger fan to the last, dull, unoriginal, and geographically uninformed. Pope hails from the tiny town of Library, Pennsylvania, in foul territory.

I countered, brilliantly, "Hit it to the catcher, Pope," a daring move on my part because the last time I had so challenged a hitter, Wertz tripled over Mueller's head.

Pope walked.

The woman in the red hat grunted audibly, for my benefit, I think, and the man behind me, that invisible specter said, "All right, Bill boy, hit 'er a mile."

My head snapped down. I did not know any "Bill boy" in the lineup at that moment. But the specter was right.

145

There was a large gentleman stepping into the batter's box reserved for left-handed hitters, so I knew Hegan was leaving the game. The public address announcer then informed us that the new man was Bill Glynn, number 6, a 195-pound swinger who is usually inserted for defensive purposes at first base, but who has been known to hit long balls.

On this occasion, Glynn let Grissom get two strikes over, and then took a half-hearted swipe at a waist-high screwball, the pitch breaking below and away from his bat and into Westrum's happy mitt.

But the Indian inning was not over, even with Glynn's timely strikeout. Still to be subdued was the courageous Mr. Lemon, tired certainly by now, and battling what was a running tide of fortune.

Lemon—like Maglie—did what he could do, and he did it well. Hitting left handed (as do so many Indians) he stroked a line drive at Whitey Lockman that the Giant first baseman caught before the crowd could fairly begin its gasp or its cheer, and the half-inning was over.

In the Giant tenth, the Indians were down to a substitute first baseman, a substitute shortstop, a substitute right fielder, and a substitute catcher. Their regular center fielder and third baseman, Doby and Rosen, were badly hobbled by injuries that certainly must have become more painful as the game progressed.

And on the mound was a tired, very courageous gentleman who had gone to the limit of his strength and resources and, like other courageous gentlemen, would go a little farther.

The Giants, on the other hand, had not removed a man from their starting lineup with the exception of their pitching. And here they were fresh, with more strength and talent in the bullpen in case it should be needed.

Don Mueller was the first Giant hitter in the bottom of the tenth inning, and I nudged the man on my right—perfectly correct etiquette, he was a Giant fan, though a Cadillac-lover—and I said, "Watch Mueller really pole one."

Mueller was apparently not doing any slap hitting today. He was taking a full-arm swing and pulling the ball to right field. Twice he had singled, and it was obvious to me that he had Lemon's number.

So Lemon reached in and found some more strength and struck Mueller out, a rare feat because Don strikes out less often than any other major-league regular.

When Mueller swung and missed the third strike, the catcher dropped the ball and had to tag the batter at the plate. It was then that I realized there had been a change in Indian catchers. Apparently I hadn't heard the announcer tell of the substitution, or else I had assumed the new catcher had to be Hal Naragon, the only other catcher beside Hegan on my scorecard.

To verify the change so that my scorecard would be complete and correct for posterity, I asked the man on my right, "Who's that catching? Naragon?"

He said, "I didn't catch the name. Didn't sound like Naragon."

I looked back at my program. Number 18, Hal Naragon, catcher. No other catcher was listed. But Naragon is described in the program notes as six feet tall, and this new man seemed shorter, not that athletes' statistics are any more to be believed than starlets' bust measurements. I would wager (not money, of course) that the average basketball player in the National Basketball Association is an inch-and-a-half to two inches shorter than his listing. That's how it was when I was in college, the six-footers were all described as 6′2″ and the 5′11″ men as just

147

shading six feet. (This was before the present-day epoch of seven-footers who probably aren't an inch over six-ten.)

A voice from four or five rows away cleared the mystery. "Grasso," he announced. "Mickey Grasso. That's who it is."

I remembered a man named Grasso who used to catch in the Giant organization. He was not carried on my program —a program I had begun by disliking and soon started hating because whatever I marked down for Cleveland went right through the paper and appeared on the Giant page, as though there was carbon paper between the pages. Every inning I had to erase those markings.

The other catcher, Hal Naragon, *was* carried on my souvenir program, blurbed by some Indian public-relations man as the "understudy for Hegan." Hegan had allowed himself to be quoted on Naragon—"the best-looking young catcher I have seen in a long time." Al Lopez must not have read the souvenir program, or else he did not want a young catcher, because he chose Grasso to be Hegan's understudy in this instance.

If Naragon throws as poorly as did Grasso in that fateful tenth inning, Hegan's job is secure for many years.

But I am jumping the gun.

First, Willie Mays, with one out. Willie had not made a hit in three official bats. Once he had walked. In the inning he walked, the Giants scored two runs.

Now he walked again.

Swiftly, the final two climaxes were achieved. With Mays leading off first, I whispered to the man on my left, the casino player who from time to time read his newspaper during the game, "He's going to go down."

It was not a case of omniscience. Nothing else would have made sense. The winning run had to be moved around; with Mays on second, a base hit by either of the next two batters would undoubtedly win the game. Mays just had to try to steal second.

And on what I recall as the first pitch to the next batter, Henry Thompson, and which one newspaper said was the second pitch, Mays did indeed break for second base. The center fielder is a swift runner and in the outfield gets a quicker start than anybody else alive, but he is not rated as a terribly clever base stealer. Most good base stealers do their stealing on the pitcher. That is, they make their move for second base well before the pitcher delivers the ball to the plate, yet not so soon that the pitcher is still in his suspended balk motion, the ball in front of him, belt high. In this position, the pitcher still has the option of throwing to first base, or stepping off the slab of rubber on the mound and wiping his brow.

Because of the propensity of pitchers for doing the latter, or for holding the ball so long at their belt buckles that the batters become tired of waiting and step out of the batter's box to wipe *their* brows, ball games last much longer than they did in the old days.

I noted on page nine in the souvenir program the box scores of four ball games (all won by the Giants; you can guess who put out the program) played forty or more years ago. The longest game of the four lasted one hour and forty minutes. Even as late as 1936, the Giants were beating the Braves (so the program told me) in a ten-inning contest that took an hour and fifty-five minutes.

We had been watching this game for three hours when Mays started for second, breaking for the base well after Lemon had committed himself to pitch to the plate. I hoped that somehow, despite his poor start, he would make it.

Behind the plate, Grasso leaped out of his squatting

post, the ball snatched from his big mitt by his right hand. The substitute shortstop, Sam Dente, hovered at second base. Grasso threw hurriedly, the ball bouncing about fifteen feet in front of second and coming up to Dente about shoulder high. The bounce so slowed the ball that Mays was easily able to slide in safely. Dente did not even attempt a tag.

The next day's papers informed me that the steal was not ordered by Manager Durocher, but was Mays' own idea. Mays said he noticed that Grasso did not make the usual peg to second base on Lemon's last warmup pitch before the Giant half-inning opened. He concluded that Grasso had a lame arm.

All this may be so, but I can scarcely believe that Durocher had no part in the proceedings. Possibly Mays shot Durocher a "May I take thirty giant steps?" signal, just as Durocher was preparing to shoo the young man down to second anyway. But no matter who deserves the credit (Grasso, probably), Mays ended up on second, and the next moves were apparent before they were made.

Here was the *raison d'être* for Mays' steal. Henry Thompson, who follows Mays and who had made a slashing hit in the third inning to drive in the second Giant run, would have to be given an intentional base on balls to set the stage for a possible force play at either second or third, or a double play that would end the inning—and force me to start marking the eleventh inning on the top and bottom margins of the program.

The walk to Thompson would nominally bring Irvin to the plate, but in just this situation, pinch hitter Jim Rhodes would certainly be called on. Rhodes, who is called Dusty because all ball players and most little boys named Rhodes are called Dusty, is a left-handed hitter and granted by most authorities to be baseball's best

150

pinch hitter. His particular talent is to hit line drives into the upper deck of the nearby right-field stands, not far from the foul line, though once in a while he fails to pull the ball and it ends up instead in the right-field bullpen, about four hundred and thirty feet from the plate.

This time when Thompson *had* been walked and Irvin removed from the lineup, Rhodes neither hit a line drive into the upper deck nor a ball into the bullpen.

On Lemon's first pitch—a curve ball that Lemon later insisted was a good one, but which came in at two-thirds speed on the inside corner between the waist and the shoulders—Rhodes contented himself with smiting the ball just as far as was needed.

The ball rose over the first baseman's head in a lazy arc and started to come down in the general vicinity of the right-field fence, near the foul line. The ball appeared to lag in the air, probably because its natural tendency was obeisance to the law of gravity but the wind was operating against that tendency, hustling it on, and second baseman Avila and substitute right fielder Pope rushed toward the spot where they thought it might land.

This observer insists—at this point—on a few words about Rhodes' blow and the wind.

This wind of September 29, 1954 was not a hurricane or even a strong autumnal gust. It was a perfectly ordinary wind that had the flags blown out a bit, but not tautly, and it was not the sort of wind where you grab your best hat and hang on. It was just a wind, and if I have to guess its velocity from those flags and from the way other fly balls had acted in innings past, I'd estimate it at fifteen or eighteen miles an hour, twenty at the maximum.

So when Avila says—as he did that afternoon—that he fully expected to catch the Rhodes hit, and that he

151

would have caught it if the wind had not pushed it so far away—I say, "Sore loser!"

Had there been no wind, that ball hit by Rhodes would have landed at the foot of the right-field wall, between Avila and Pope. Avila did not come within twenty feet of the ball. With no wind, he might have cut the distance in half. Pope never could have made the catch, of course, because he came as close as he did only *because* of the wind's pushing the ball further into right field. With no wind, Pope would not even have launched his futile leap at the wall.

And if I am right—as I am—the untouched fly ball, landing near the fence and near the foul line, would have carried Mays in from second base with the Giants' third run, and the ball game.

But there *was* a wind, and so Pope came closer to catching the ball than he otherwise would, flinging his body at the wall, his glove thrust high into the air. The ball, in total disregard of so majestic a leap, finished its downward arc above and to the right of Pope's head, striking some object in the first row of seats and bounding back onto the field.

Larry Napp, the umpire assigned to handle the right-field foul line, a luxury tolerated only in All-Star games and World Series contests, did not give the usual sign for a home run. Instead he made it apparent that the ball had first gone into the stands before bouncing out by holding out his left arm and then using his right hand to describe an arc over the extended arm, much like a tennis lob passing over the net. To make sure everybody understood, he repeated the gesture two or three times as he ran toward the right field wall.

It was a stroke of genius.

It also was the stroke of 4:12 p.m. And in tight procession, Mays, Thompson, and Rhodes trotted about the bases, while 52,751 paying fans, plus those countless dead heads, let loose a roar.

It was, strangely, not a gigantic all-ending roar, because too many people were in doubt as to exactly what had just transpired, and all around me I heard—yes, even among bleacher fans—"What was it, a ground-rule double?" Napp's magnificent gesture (and I am delighted to say something complimentary about an American Leaguer) had been wasted, I'm afraid.

Also, I thought I detected once more in that roar the same whooshing sound of relief, and I attributed this to the suddenly imparted knowledge that the game was over and that the thousands, hungry, tired, and stiff as myself, could now go home.

A delicious languor stole over me. I felt—with all the tiredness and the gnawing in my stomach—wonderfully, savagely happy. I looked for the woman in the red hat. She had disappeared, and I thought: good, crawl back to that rock.

I turned to look—at long last—at the man who sat behind me and rooted for Cleveland, but all I saw was a mass of shoving humanity, struggling down the aisles and over the wooden planks toward the one exit.

I shrugged. I didn't care. He was a Cleveland fan and he had suffered enough. My wife—I knew—was wrong. I am not really a vindictive person.

When my team has won.

153

AFTERWORD TO THE 2004 EDITION

Extra Innings

Half a century has passed since a baseball thrown by Don Liddle, of the New York Giants, and hit by Vic Wertz, of the Cleveland Indians, landed in the pocket of a Rawlings glove owned by one Willie Mays, of immortality. Fifty years ago on September 29, 1954.

That moment galvanized a bleacherite to write a book about that game. I was the bleacherite.

I am not a historian. I am not even a historian of baseball. I am an observer, an enthusiast. But permit me to discuss two matters. The first is obvious: where are they now, those men of autumn in Giants' uniforms? And how about the brash 32-year-old bleacherite who sat for six hours and wrote a book?

First things first. Twelve Giants appeared on the field of play that day in the old horseshoe-shaped Polo Grounds (now gone), plus manager Leo Durocher. Durocher is dead, although he lasted well into his eighty-sixth year. (Very well, indeed, judging by five marriages and two penile implants.) Likewise four of the players are dead: starting pitcher Sal Maglie; his reliever Don Liddle; catcher Wes Westrum; and third baseman Hank Thompson, the one tragic figure of the afternoon.

The others are alive at this writing, living in the main in tiny rural towns I cannot find in my world atlas: Easley, South Carolina; Farmers Branch, Texas; Hazelwood, Missouri. Baseball players spend their careers in the turbulent centers of commerce and then return to the peace of rural America.

Only Whitey Lockman lives elsewhere—in Scottsdale, Arizona. But then Lockman always had a sophisticated manner. Not only did he play the game, he coached it and managed it— for a total of fifty years in baseball. And a small moment in his managing career is a large moment in the racial makeup of baseball. On May 8, 1973, nineteen years after the first game of the 1954 World Series, Chicago Cubs manager Whitey Lockman argued with the plate umpire, who thumbed him from the game. Lockman told coach Ernie Banks to manage the rest of the game. Thus Lockman appointed the first black to manage a major league baseball team.

Because I have begun with Lockman, the first baseman that day, let me continue through the infield. David Carlous Williams—Little Davey he was called, at tiptoe five feet ten inches—had a career as brief as Lockman's was long. The year after the 1954 series, Williams called it quits because of chronic back pain. He had spent his career, all six years, with the New York Giants. Williams was a lovely infielder, covering ground with easy grace, pivoting smoothly on double plays, a man of swift reflexes and, indeed, a certain amount of luck.

I took my son Stephen, aged 11, to see his first big league game in 1955—the Giants and the Brooklyn Dodgers, baseball's best rivalry. In a late inning, after the Dodgers had loaded the bases with nobody out, Jackie Robinson lifted a pop fly into short right field. Back wheeled Davey Williams, tracking down the ball. The runners froze for a moment. Williams leaped. The ball touched the tips of his gloved fingers and bounced high into the air. The runners broke. Williams lunged for the ball and caught it just short of the grass. He whirled and threw to shortstop Alvin Dark, doubling up the runner on second, now halfway to third. Dark turned, and the runner on first was almost near enough to be tagged. Dark ran at him, the runner backtracked, and Dark flipped to Lockman. Voila, a triple play.

If Williams made little ripples with his play, Alvin Dark made waves, and later he gave new life to the old adage: big league managers never die, they're just traded away. After a rich playing career with the Boston Braves and the Giants, and three World Series where he batted .323 in sixteen games, Dark managed four different clubs. He was fired from the Giants job at the end of the 1964 season after he either did or did not say to sportswriter Stan Isaacs of *Newsday*: "We have trouble because we have so many Spanish-speaking players and Negroes on the team. They are just not able to perform up to the white players when it comes to mental attitude."

Dark would say later: "I was gravely misquoted and misinterpreted."

He may indeed have been misquoted. After all, as he said in his defense, he played black Jim Ray Hart over white Jim Davenport at third base. He played Spanish-speaking Orlando Cepeda, Jose Pagan, Juan Marichal, and all those Alou brothers. Yet a tiny moment in my presence leads to my discomfort with his defense. I was at the Giants' training camp in Phoenix in 1963, on assignment to write a profile of Dark, the Giants' manager. Dark told the press one afternoon that the Giants had signed a new pitcher, whom Dark described as six feet two, 200 pounds, with a good fastball and excellent control. Then he stopped and leaned forward and said, with a grin, "And he is black as the ace of spades."

Dark went on to manage at Kansas City, at Cleveland, and finally at Oakland, living what he called in print "a full Christian life" that "made me a better man."

In the outfield, it was Monte Irvin in left, Don Mueller in right, and Mays in center, and all are alive today. Irvin is down in Florida, taking life easy after a career—really two careers—in baseball. He spent eleven years in the Negro

157

League, very likely the best hitter in the league after Josh Gibson, the legendary catcher, and perhaps the greatest hitter of any color.

Irvin joined the Giants when he was thirty years old. Had he not gone into the Army during World War II, some people believe Branch Rickey intended to sign Irvin as the first black player in the majors. That's how good Irvin was. He twice led the Negro League in batting—in 1941, hitting an astonishing .422, and in 1946, .389. Five years later he led the National League in runs batted in. In the 1951 World Series against the Yankees, he batted .458, with a triple and two home runs. He stole home in the first inning of the first game.

Monte Irvin was born in 1919 on a sugar plantation in Columbus, Alabama, one of ten children. He attended a small black university in Pennsylvania, playing baseball in the summers with the Newark Eagles. In 1941, when he hit .422, Branch Rickey scouted him to be that first black major leaguer. Or so the story goes. When the Eagles disbanded—the Negro League began to wither soon after Jackie Robinson broke the color barrier—Irvin went south, joining a Cuban winter league. Giants scout Alex Pompez saw him and advised Horace Stoneham, the Giants' owner, to sign him to play with Jersey City, the Giants' farm team in the International League. In 1950 Irvin hit .510 in eighteen games at Jersey City, with ten home runs and thirty-three runs batted in.

What might the numbers have been in a full 154-game season—eighty homers, 250 RBIs? Cool Papa Bell, of the Negro League, said of Irvin: "Monte was one of the best young ballplayers at the time." Unfortunately his time was too soon. He was ready for baseball five years before white baseball was ready for him. Bell said Irvin would have hit "600 or 700" home runs had he come up sooner. Nobody invited him. His major league baseball career was shortened not just because he was too old when it began, but also because he shattered an ankle in a training camp game in 1952. He never ran as well.

158

He reinjured the leg in 1953, and three years later he retired. He later scouted for the Mets.

Monte Irvin was—and is—as great a man as he was a player. In 1968 he became assistant director of public relations to baseball commissioner William Eckert. He had a ball field named after him in East Orange, New Jersey. They made him father of the year in 1973 in Jersey. When he was elected to the Hall of Fame in 1973, he paid homage to the sport: "Baseball has done more to move America in the right direction than all the professional patriots with their billions of cheap words."

They called Don Mueller "Mandrake the Magician." He handled a bat the way a college majorette handles her baton or Houdini his wand. He poked hits all over, a modern Willie ("Hit 'em where they ain't") Keeler, except with more power. But power or not, he always hit the ball. One year he led the league with 212 hits. In that 1954 sweep he batted .389. It never mattered who pitched; one day Mueller hit for the cycle—single, double, triple, home run—off four different pitchers.

In 1958 the Giants sold him to the White Sox, and a year later he quit the game at age thirty-two. Like a good magician he disappeared into the woodwork or rather, to Hazelwood, Missouri.

Willie Mays was the other outfielder that day. His catch in the eighth inning, detailed in the book, made the win possible that day. Had the Giants lost, who knows what would have happened the next three games.

The greatest ballplayer of our time, many have called Mays. Some go further: the greatest player of any time.

And the catch, some say, was the greatest catch ever. But it wasn't even the greatest catch I saw Mays make. Once, in a game against Cincinnati, Bobby Tolan of the Reds drove a ball toward the right centerfield seats of Candlestick Park. Bobby Bonds—Barry's father—came racing over from right field. Mays ran to his left, from center. At a point in the air, the ball,

159

Bonds, Mays, and the fence converged in a terrific collision. Bobby Bonds rose quickly and looked for the ball. Had it gone over the fence? Did it lie somewhere on the grass?

The ball lay in Mays's glove. Bonds plucked the ball from the glove and held it up for all to see.

And another Mays catch was even better. The date was September 4, 1964, ten years after the catch against Cleveland. In the fourth inning with two outs, the Giants leading 1–0 at Connie Mack Stadium, the Phillies' John Callison punched a single to left field. Ruben Amaro, a Punch-and-Judy hitter who seldom drove the ball any real distance, came up. Mays played Amaro the way he played poke hitters—so close he looked like another infielder. Amaro hit probably the longest ball he had ever hit to the opposite field, a curling drive headed for the scoreboard in right centerfield at the 385-foot marker.

Mays whirled and ran. He leaped, left hand extended. He grabbed the ball with that extended gloved hand and threw his legs straight out so he wouldn't hit the fence with his face. He hit it with his legs in a fearful smash. His body bent like a diver's off the high board in a back dive. He crashed to the ground and lay still.

"For a moment," he would say later, "I thought I was hurt. Bad. Then I knew I wasn't." He danced up, flipped the ball to rightfielder Jim Ray Hart, and the Philadelphia crowd, not known for its generosity to a rival player, stood and roared. The stadium buzzed for two innings. In the clubhouse, Phils' manager Gene Mauch said, "The only way you can make a better catch is under your armpit."

Willie Mays played too long. He should have quit before he was traded, at his request, to the Mets in 1972. He wanted to wind up his career in New York. But he was forty-one years old, and it was a mistake. In the World Series the next season, against Oakland, Mays swung at a pitched ball and topped it, headed back to the mound. Mays fell down from the swing. He got up and started to run and fell down again. He also fell

160

down on the basepaths that day. He fell down chasing a base hit. Mays was astonished in the locker room when reporters asked him kindly and gently about what was going on. "Did I look that bad?" he wanted to know. He looked worse. He didn't look like Willie Mays.

I prefer to overlook those two years. Stan Musial had called Mays "the perfect ballplayer." No one ever said it better.

One outfielder on the Giants' roster didn't play in the field that day. He just came in to take a swipe at the ball in a pinch-hitting appearance in the tenth inning. His name was Dusty Rhodes. More correctly James Lamar Rhodes, except that boys named Rhodes often end up Dusty. Dusty Rhodes described himself this way: "I can't field and I've got a lousy arm, but I sure love to whack at that ball."

That fateful year, 1954, Rhodes hit fifteen home runs, most of them in pinch-hitting appearances. When he wasn't hitting base-balls, he was hitting the bottle. It came naturally. He once said of his father, "He was a corn farmer. He raised 200 gallons."

You know what Dusty did the first time he whacked at a ball in the 1954 World Series. He hit a home run. The next day, the Giants trailing 1–0, he popped a single into short centerfield to tie the game. Later that day he got behind a pitch and belted it on a rising line onto the roof of the rightfield stands to win the game. His pinch single off Mike Garcia helped win the third game. In those three games he went four for six, with two home runs. The Indians finally got him out in that third game. The first page photo of *The New York Times* the next day showed Rhodes striking out. That was news. Rhodes sat out the fourth game, laughing at the hapless Indians. Rhodes's four hits in three games had driven in seven runs. The Indians scored just five runs as a team those three games.

When the Giants moved to San Francisco, they left Dusty behind. He didn't need the chi-chi city on the Bay. He went home, making occasional command appearances to talk about the old days when nobody whacked at the ball better.

161

Three pitchers worked that day in 1954: Sal Maglie, Don Liddle, and grizzled Marv Grissom.

If Dusty Rhodes was a light and joyful figure, Maglie was dark and somber. They called him the Barber. I had always thought that was because he liked to shave the batters with his fast stuff under the chin. I am told he was the Barber long before, having swept out barbershops in his home town of Niagara Falls.

Maglie pitched ten years in the majors, after a brief whirl with the Mexican League, where he'd gone because nobody in the big leagues wanted him. Maglie had no real overpowering stuff. But he always had courage and he had brains. If he couldn't throw a ball past a hitter, his nasty slider induced hitters to dribble harmless ground balls.

A year after the 1954 World Series, the Giants traded Sal Maglie to the hated Dodgers, a team Maglie had beaten like a drum. In September 1956, he tossed a no-hitter for the Dodgers against the Phillies, winning 5–0. He found himself on October 8, 1956, starting another World Series contest, against the Yankees.

I sat in the rightfield mezzanine that day at Yankee Stadium. Maglie was then thirty-nine years old. Two years earlier he had worked into the eighth inning before coach Freddie Fitzsimmons handed the ball to Don Liddle. Now once again Maglie pitched into the eighth inning. Nobody had to relieve him. All he did in that eighth inning was strike out pitcher Don Larsen, strike out Hank Bauer, strike out Joe Collins. His only problem was that Don Larsen had chosen this day to throw his immortal perfect game, twenty-seven Dodgers up and down. The Yankees won 2–0. And soon Maglie was out of baseball.

In 1982 he suffered the first of three strokes in a five-year stretch. He lived through them. But a bronchial infection became pneumonia in 1992, and he died three days after Christmas, seventy-five years old.

162

The baseball Freddie Fitzsimmons took from Sal Maglie in 1954 was handed to Don Liddle, the lefthander whose job was to retire left-handed-hitting Vic Wertz. Liddle threw one pitch. Wertz hit it 462 feet to Willie Mays, and Liddle left the ball field. Later his obituary would write that Liddle had said of that one pitch, "Well, I got my man." I doubt he said it, but it makes a nice story.

Liddle's career and life make nice, and true, stories. Liddle pitched the last game of that 1954 Series, with the Giants beating the bejeebers out of Bob Lemon for a 7–0 lead. The Giants eventually won 7–4, Liddle pitching six and two-third innings for the win.

Liddle had come to the Giants after seven seasons in the minors and a year with the Braves. In 1953 he was involved in the trade that sent Giants hero Bobby Thomson to the Braves, with John Antonelli coming to the Giants. Liddle was a sort of throw-in. In the next two seasons, Liddle won nineteen games and lost eight. Some throw-in. The Giants then traded him to the Cardinals, and two years later he retired to be with family in Mt. Carmel, Illinois. He bought a gas station; sold it and went into insurance; and from there moved to a tool factory, where he worked for twenty-two years. He died of cancer in 2000, at age seventy-five, leaving his wife and four sons and a daughter, and one World Series ring. Plus a moment of fame when he threw one pitch to Vic Wertz. It all worked out nicely.

It worked out nicely because Marv Grissom picked up the pieces in that eighth inning, Indians on first and third and one out. Grissom walked a pinch-hitter, then struck out the next pinch-hitter and retired catcher Jim Hegan on a long fly ball. No runs. No runs for the full two and two-third innings he worked that afternoon.

Grissom pitched for the Giants through 1958, and then for St. Louis, and continued his career as a coach and scout. Grissom was a big man, six foot three, 230 pounds. He had a blazing fastball when he broke in, and when that fizzled out, he developed a screwball, curving the ball away from left-handed hitters. But mainly he had what the kids today call attitude. Sportswriter Leonard Koppett summed up Grissom: "An old hardbitten power pitcher . . . who never set the world on fire but also had the perfect reliever's mental toughness."

Grissom established a National League record for pitchers, with 219 consecutive errorless games over a nearly five-year span. And he could pitch. With the Giants from 1954 through 1957, these are his earned-run averages: 2.36, 2.93, 1.56, and 2.60. In 1954 he appeared in fifty-six games. He won ten and saved nineteen others. He couldn't have saved many more because the Giants also had as a reliever Hoyt Wilhelm, who was probably the very best in baseball during those years. But Wilhelm's fluttering knuckle ball could not be trusted with a man on third in a later inning, as the Indians had that day. The pitch might have escaped catcher Wes Westrum, and the lead run would have scored. So it was Grissom. Nobody scored.

Grissom spent twenty-plus years in baseball. He is today, at eighty-six, the senior Giant alive from that 1954 team.

Wesley Noreen Westrum caught all those pitches that day, and most every day. Westrum may have been the worst-hitting regular in the National League the years he played with the Giants. That was odd because he came up as a power-hitting catcher. When he joined the Giants in 1949, he'd hit five bases-loaded home runs in fifty-one games at Jersey City. Men don't hit five grand slams in entire careers. Durocher could not wait to thrust him into the starting lineup. Westrum didn't care to play that soon. He had a broken finger on his throwing hand, an injury he hadn't planned to reveal until it had passed. He had no choice. He said to Durocher, "My right forefinger is broken. What do you want me to do?" Durocher not only believed nice guys finished last, he also felt you played the game under any burden whatsoever. "Tape it and run dirt over the tape," he said curtly. "Then get out and catch Jansen."

164

He did. Larry Jansen threw a three-hit shutout to the man with a broken finger.

Westrum's reputation as a hitter receded as his fielding reputation grew. In 1950 he committed just one error in 139 games, for a .999 average, a record that stood for forty-seven years before Charles Johnson broke it in an errorless season. Westrum's career batting average was .217. Some pitchers hit higher than that. It never mattered. He was an All-Star in 1952 and 1953, not because of his bat.

After the Giants moved to San Francisco, Westrum coached the team, and in July 1965 he became the manager of the stumbling New York Mets, chosen ahead of Yogi Berra. He brought the right temperament to the job. After all, he had managed a team during World War II at a disciplinary barracks in Greenhaven, New York. "A place for difficult cases," he would say later. "It was good training for the Mets."

Nothing was good training for the Mets. Westrum quit in 1967, citing "physical and mental strain." All that losing. He rejoined the Giants, managing the team in 1974, and wound up scouting for the Atlanta Braves. He spent nearly thirty years in professional ball.

Cancer struck him down at age seventy-nine, in Clearbrook, Minnesota.

Which leaves only Hank Thompson of those men of autumn. His was the most autumnal life of all. Too small to play major league baseball, at five foot eight and 160 pounds when the season started and less than 150 pounds when it ended, he looked like a junior high player. Yet sometimes he batted cleanup for the Giants, hitting screaming line drives into the rightfield seats, three in one game against the Cards, and two inside-the-park home runs in another game, the first National Leaguer to do that in fourteen years.

His father had beaten him with a strap when Hank didn't obey him fast enough, the boy lying naked under the lashing. Hank spent time in a reform school, a euphemism for a penitentiary for wayward kids. No matter what, he managed to play ball; it was his escape.

By age fifteen he had joined the great Kansas City Monarchs—Satchel Paige's team—the very best team in the Negro League. He not only started to drink with the Monarchs, he began to carry a gun. "It made me feel like a man," he told me later.

In 1954 Thompson received the winner's share of $11,147.90, the largest World Series take at the time. What he didn't give away of the money, he drank away. With the Giants he had found what the shrinks call an "enabler," a person who becomes the drinker's drinking buddy, a conspirator in Thompson's illness and march toward oblivion. The buddy was Giants' owner Horace Stoneham. Stoneham would phone Thompson to come to his office. Thompson did as he was told. Stoneham locked the door and took out a bottle and two glasses.

There was a difference, of course. Stoneham was a white multimillionaire who could dry out at expensive, secluded clinics. Thompson was a working stiff, and black.

Not that Stoneham didn't help. That's what buddies are for. One off-season Thompson killed a man in a fight. The man, Buddy Crowe, pulled a knife on Thompson. "Moneybags," he called out to Thompson. "I'm going to get you." Thompson had once seen Buddy Crowe use his knife to tear out the entrails of another man in another drinking brawl.

Thompson yelled "Stop!" as Crowe approached him. Crowe didn't stop until Thompson had shot him. Three times. The next day Stoneham and the Giants got him off on a dropped charge. Self-defense, everybody agreed. Thompson knew better. "I could have run," he said to me. "I didn't have to shoot him."

Next Thompson held up a bar in Harlem with a gun. The bartender called the cops, who picked up Hank a few doors down. Thompson grinned a wide grin into the camera of a *New*

166

York Daily News photographer. "I guess I was glad I was caught."

Enablers don't let you stay caught. Stoneham got him off again. Finally Thompson took an armed revolver into a liquor store in Dallas and left with $200 and a bottle of Scotch. This time it was too late. Thompson was no longer any use to the Giants. Nobody intervened. Perhaps nobody could have. Thompson received a ten-year sentence, served five, and came out of the Huntsville facility bone dry. He moved to Fresno to live with his mother. He landed a job as playground director of the Parks and Recreation Department of Fresno. He went to church. He attended AA meetings. He never touched a drop. He passed bars and walked around drunks lying on the streets. No matter. A heart attack dropped him on a Fresno street. He was dead on arrival at a VA hospital.

How good a ballplayer had he been? A wonderful player. When he was healthy and strong, he could hit the ball a mile; he could fly around the bases. He fielded his position at third base as well as any third baseman in the league. He set a league record for double plays at third in one season. In the 1954 World Series he hit safely in every game, batted .364, scored six runs.

He was the second black player, after Larry Doby, to be signed by an American League team, the St. Louis Browns. St. Louis was probably the worst city, outside of Philadelphia, for a black player in those days. The Browns used him as an attendance gimmick. They would announce he would start as a second baseman the first game of a forthcoming series. He would play before a large crowd, and then sit out the rest of the series. At the end of that first season, the Browns fired him. "How come?" Thompson wanted to know. "I had a better year than a lot of other guys on this team." He had. But he was black. That was enough.

I make no excuses for his behavior. No other black ballplayer, back then, had shot another man to death. No other

167

black player had drunk himself into prison after two armed holdups. He did what he did. But he also spent his time. He was on his way to redemption. He never touched another drop after he left Huntsville.

Too late. Too late. Tragedy ought to be ennobling. In Hank's case it was just sad. He lies in Odd Fellows Cemetery in Fresno.

Those are the men of autumn.

❖   ❖   ❖

Now, at age eighty-two, I tell my son about baseball games I saw back then and remind him of the day we sat and watched a triple play unfold. In turn he sends me clips that once in a while mention my name. "What will baseball be like," he asks rhetorically, "when you and Ray Robinson and all those other old guys are dead?" My son is a morbid sort, as you can tell.

But the question is good. What will it be like? Not much different, despite those ridiculous salaries and the ridiculous cost of hot dogs in the ballpark. Let me return for a moment to the Rawlings glove of Willie Mays with which I began these extra innings.

Don Liddle, who threw that pitch that wound up in Mays's glove (a glove once described as "the place where triples go to die"), brought his son Craig to the Giants' clubhouse on a later date so the boy could meet his idol, Willie Mays. Willie and the six-year-old boy chatted briefly, and Mays then asked, "Do you need a new glove?"

The boy who would soon enter Little League nodded his blond head. Mays took a glove and handed it to the youngster. "Take care of this," Mays said solemnly, "and it will take care of you."

The boy took the glove, not knowing he now owned *the* glove of *that* catch. When his dad told him, Craig insisted on putting the glove in a safe deposit box at the local bank. Later, when the glove would no longer be much too big for his hand, he took it out of the bank and used it through his sandlot years. Craig then sent the glove on loan to the Baseball Hall of Fame Museum in Cooperstown, New York, where it now lies, a jewel among the museum's other priceless jewels.

Baseball, for all its faults, for its lopsided leagues and its towering salaries, for all its drug use and its daily docket of crime, for its loss of balance, still remains our greatest game. It is also the simplest.

It so often comes down to a boy, his baseball glove, and a hero.

Arnold Hano
Laguna Beach, California